♡

Vivien —

This book is my ♡ present for you. I was when I wrote it, I was also in my process of understanding life, learning and teaching and learning again and again... life is a process that unfolds... you will get it just as I did

Love
Lorraine

January 5/21

ENLIGHTENMENT DANCE
How Dance Can Improve the Way You Think, Feel, and Live

Rosane Gibson

authorHOUSE

AuthorHouse™
1663 Liberty Drive
Bloomington, IN 47403
www.authorhouse.com
Phone: 1 (800) 839-8640

© 2006 Rosane Gibson. All rights reserved.

Author photo by Bruce Hallgarth
Cover art by Holly Sierra – www.HollySierra.com
Inside art work by Carla Lim, Alexia Lim, Sasha Lim and Kristina Olson

No part of this book may be reproduced, stored in a retrieval system, or transmitted by any means without the written permission of the author.

Published by AuthorHouse 06/27/2019

ISBN: 978-1-7283-1623-9 (hc)
ISBN: 978-1-4678-0070-9 (e)

Library of Congress Control Number: 2006903871

Print information available on the last page.

Any people depicted in stock imagery provided by Getty Images are models, and such images are being used for illustrative purposes only. Certain stock imagery © Getty Images.

This book is printed on acid-free paper.

Because of the dynamic nature of the Internet, any web addresses or links contained in this book may have changed since publication and may no longer be valid. The views expressed in this work are solely those of the author and do not necessarily reflect the views of the publisher, and the publisher hereby disclaims any responsibility for them.

TABLE OF CONTENTS

DEDICATION vii

ACKNOWLEGEMENTS ix

PREFACE xi

ABOUT THE AUTHOR xiii

OVERVIEW OF CONTENTS xix

INTRODUCTION 1

ENLIGHTENING THE MIND 13

ENLIGHTENING THE SOUL 45

MOVEMENT & PRESENTATION 67

TELLING STORIES THROUGH DANCE 81

ENLIGHTENING THE BODY 137

BE IN THE MOMENT 147

ENLIGHTENMENT DANCE STUDENTS' STORIES 159

BIBLIOGRAPHY 169

ABOUT THE AUTHOR 171

DEDICATION

To my three sons, Werner, Renan and Rolf.
Thanks for dancing with me!

ACKNOWLEGEMENTS

Special thanks to **my mother Maria Stella da Cunha e Souza** for signing me up in dance classes at early ages. **Dance Master Adnan Sarhan, Gabrielle Roth, Amel Tafsout, Janeeda, Fatima Fontes and Regina Ferrari** for teaching me that dance is a matter of the spirit. **Mestre Lazaro** for being a role model of an inspiring teacher. **Dance Teacher Jehan** for singing upon my Goddess within. **Dance Teacher Julianne Battaglia** for inspiration and creativity. **Dance Teacher Morocco** for knowledge and tradition. **Dance Teacher Pat Ford "Najla"** for costuming ideas and friendship. **Dance Teacher Amara Al Amir** for ideas and support. **Dance Teacher Amiramor** for caring and charisma. **Lonny Brown** for awakening my chakras through enlightening writings and being a best friend and editor. **Harold Cober** for being my spiritual guru and advisor and for helping me unveiling the mysteries of the unknown. **Janet Payne** for being my right arm on all projects I ventured, a student, a teacher, a sister and an artist of many forms. **Sylvia Partain** for inspiring me with wisdom and sympathy. **Cindy Marks** for believing in the Enlightenment Dance project and opening doors for me. **Christine Praria** for being a perfect student, the one who overcomes the master, and for reviewing and advising for this book. **Angela Renton, Anna Baildon, Tereza Gomes, Cacilda Andrade "Estrela", Lucy Lipstick, Christine Praria, Sherry McDonald, Carla Lim, Lisa Myers "Lilith" and Deborah Gross** for supporting and promoting my dance classes and workshops. Special thanks to my students **Carla, Alexia** and **Sasha Lim** and to **Kristina Olson** for the beautiful drawings. **David Snyder** for being a patient talented photographer. **Deborah Snyder** and daughters **Alana** and **Gabriel** for cheering and embracing Enlightenment Dance and myself. **Karen Andes** for inspiring me to be a writer. **Ronaldo Brazil** for the beautiful cover art. **Zhenia Nicholles** for being my soul sister and awakening my Gypsy within. **Andrew Guilfoil "Zhor"** for sharing sacred dance dreams and becoming my dance partner. **Nichole Hein** for taking off on the Enlightenment Dance Project, helping teaching classes and assisting on events. **Kimberly Hanson** for being a friend and for embracing Enlightenment Dance as a path of healing. **Conrad Tillman** for helping with the final editing and publishing of this book. The **Sauer Brothers** (my sons) for being my support team for whatever crosses my mind and of course, for dancing with me. All my students that inspired me throughout the years, and for you, reader, who have been always in my mind.

PREFACE

Warning: This book is not for "you..."

.. at least not for the part of you that blindly believes, and waits for a miracle to improve your life..

It is certainly not for any part of you that thinks you are better than me, or that I am better than you!

And, this book is not for the "you" that thinks you are not already enlightened. It is surly not for any part of you that believes you cannot dance!

I wrote this book for the true essence of you; the part that already "knows." It is for your higher consciousness, the part that wants to play with your inner wisdom, the eternal child of the Universe.

The words and ideas in this book are for the part of you that says YES to life, that already knows me and my message. That part is awake in the here and now, at this very moment and knows that you and I are already enlightened.

I write to the part of you that can dance... not the "you" that you think you know, but for the YOU that knows more than you know!

And I write for me too; for the part of me that is just like the part of you that we don't yet know. You think this book is about dance, but there is a part of us that knows that it is more: The Enlightenment Dance that is performed at every movement by the timeless rhythm of the Universe.

May the divine part of me that knows, greet the divine part of you that also knows. May they dance together the Dance of Eternal Bliss and enjoy the message behind the words in this book.

Rosane Gibson

(..flying at 30 thousand feet, from New York to Orlando, Feb. 2003)

ABOUT THE AUTHOR

I was born to the rhythms of Samba. In Brazil everyone dances!

Music always fascinated me. I grew up watching my aunty Regina dancing. She was so full of energy!

My family was huge: I had 13 cousins, 6 uncles, my mother Stella, my sister Eliane, and aunty Regina. We used to gather at my grandmother's big house for every celebration. I remember our Christmas gatherings where I would always get my cousins and sister involved in an artistic project. One day I made everyone act in a theater play that I had written. We made up costumes with curtains and sheet pieces from my grandma's closet. The play ended up with carnival dancing! Aunty Regina always danced with me and I wanted to be like her. My mother used to dress me up in dance costumes for the Brazilian Carnival parties, and I loved it! I became Ballerina, Carmen Miranda, Hawaiian Girl, and "Baiana".

I remember dancing around my living room at the age of three. My mother enrolled me in ballet classes when I was just five. When I was eleven, I was dancing in point shoes and dreaming of becoming a famous ballerina. My ballet teacher introduced me to several creative routines fusing Jazz and modern dance. I was really fascinated by the Belly Dance number she once created! I danced with veils and dressed like a harem princess!

I wanted to do more of that dance, but it was just a single performance. How enchanting, and how sad that I would not be able to do it again (at least for a long time)!

My mother took me out of the dance classes when we had financial difficulties and she could not afford them. She didn't know how hard this impacted me! I promised myself that one day, somehow, I would be a famous ballerina and would travel the whole world sharing my dance.

Time went by, I grew up, I married and I had kids. Like many of us, my dream of becoming a ballerina was overshadowed by my busy life. It was only when I got divorced that my life unfolded into a path of self-discovery and healing. I got involved in mind, body and spirit philosophies. I read many books in psychology, self-improvement and ecology.

I could never get used to the uncaring violence and chaos in the world. I always thought somebody had to do something to change it, so I took initiatives by participating in movements for peace and coordinating environmental projects. I wanted a better world for my sons and their friends! In between parenting and going to College, I studied theater and poetry, and had weekly therapy sessions for over two years. I worked at Varig Brazilian Airlines and then British Airways at the Rio de Janeiro Airport for several years. The jobs in aviation made me a student of human emotions, watching so many travelers: happy to go somewhere, sad about leaving a loved one, angry because of the delays, fearful of flying or feeling compassionate towards someone else; a lot of deep emotions!

I have always been fascinated with airplanes and travel. I love to pack and go! I love to meet new people and to be able to be on the other side of the Planet in just few hours. I also love to see different cultures and learn from them. But what mostly fascinates me is flying. The fluffy shapes of the clouds, the rainbows, the stars and even the turbulence on the airplane reminds me of a dance in the sky! So, I became a Flight Attendant.

One day I went to the doctor because I was feeling back pain and he said to me that all I needed was to exercise. I told him I hated to exercise and that nothing really appealed to me but to dance. So, he said, *dance every day! Do it! This is your exercise; take it seriously!*

In 1995, I left Brazil and lived in England for two years. I made many friends in the paradise-like Isle of Wight where I had the opportunity to start teaching the dance that I would later call "Enlightenment Dance." My classes were held in St Thomas's, a Victorian Gothic church in Newport. It was so spiritual to hear the bells in the 138-foot tower ringing at the start of our dance sessions! I remember when I drove my bicycle around the Island hanging up class flyers at the stores and making friends with the locals. Those classes became very popular on this English island and my flyers attracted several enlightened students. Among these, Angela Renton and Anna Baildon became close friends. I found out that by teaching dance I was connecting to the Brazilian part of me that was starving for the fun and spontaneous dance I used to see everywhere in my home country.

A year later I had to move to America, and we were all very sad because we thought those fun dance classes were coming to an end. But that was not an end; it was just the beginning of an enlightening journey! I encouraged Angela to keep teaching the classes and so she did! In my small house at Newport, I taught Angela everything I knew and she took notes and recorded videos. From there we parted, but remained in close contact. My little dance school still blooms on English soil! Angela established a spiritual approach to manage the funding of the classes. The money collected is kept in a savings account for the benefit of the group. They use it to buy costumes, to pay for teachers to come and present workshops, or for any performance needs. Every now and then I go back and teach and share new discoveries of Enlightenment Dance, and feel inspired by the feedback I get from my sisters there!

Enlightenment Dance really came into existence after the drastic events of September 11,th 2001. Working as a Flight Attendant for American Airlines, I was based in New York City at the time and I felt like I was seeing terrorism too up-close. It was really not fun, and I decided that I wanted to stop flying. This decision killed me inside, because flying was what I loved! By flying I connect with the world, I expand my dancing horizons by meeting other dancers, learning and teaching in the cities that I visit. I would take people to their destinations, and would have access to the world!

The Company offered leave of absence, and I was grounded for six months. During this time, I was able to transmute my fear by elaborating the concepts and definitions of my Enlightenment Dance Company. I made the web page and started this book. In this process the Flight Attendant Dance Choreography creatively came to my mind. By depicting events in flight, and the airliner environment, I was both dancing and healing myself and others. Much of this book was written while I was literally miles high in the sky, flying at hundreds of miles per hour, so I have shared flight information with you at the ends of those sections.

The first title of this book was "Inner Ecology," because I switched my attention from environmental health to the inner path of self-discovery and healing. I figured out that the world is like a big engine and the only way to fix it up is by fixing ourselves first. Here I am, writing on the plane at 35 thousand feet, with my laptop wirelessly connected to the world. It is fascinating, isn't it?

As my scientist friend Harold Cober says, wireless connection is the first step before telepathic communications. I hope you will be able to receive my telepathic inputs from these pages, like a wireless connection, heart to heart! Consume it, then re-think your life, and dance! The message within has helped me discover enlightenment, and it will help you too!

May the world be in Bliss!

With love, Rosane

(..somewhere over the Atlantic Ocean, Winter, 2003)

OVERVIEW OF CONTENTS

Hello dear reader!

I believe that we are cosmically connected, even though we might not know each other. Our minds cross the "barrier" of time and space and we are *here* in the *now*, sharing the exciting message of this book about Enlightenment Dance. Of course it is not the ultimate truth about enlightenment or dance or anything else, but it is the result of my own experience and learning process, which I feel so moved to share with you.

I like to use the "shopping" analogy. When we go shopping, we see several products on the shelves, but we don't buy them all! Some of them we know are not good for us, so we leave them on the shelf. Others are worth a try, so we take them home. There are products that we have already experienced and we know for sure that they are good, so we buy lots of them. There are others that, although good, may be unaffordable, so we leave without them. Please do the same here! Take what you think is good for you. During your "cosmic" shopping for inspiration or truth, take with you what makes sense and leave what doesn't. You may come back later for a better understanding of some concepts, or maybe you will come up with a totally different idea!

The first part of the book is a brief overview of the history of the dance, along with an explanation of the word "enlightenment" and the concept of Enlightenment Dance. I also explain the benefits of Enlightenment Dancing for the body, mind and soul. The second part is getting started on the *dance of the thoughts* and learning to transmute feelings and sensations by becoming more aware of your emotions. I start some chapters with dictionary definitions to clarify some key concepts. I suggest some dance exercises to guide you through a formless Dance Meditation, and Ecstatic Dancing. Then we go on a Body & Mind & Soul journey, to learn about the energy centers of the body and their subtle connections. I invite you to bring the ancient oriental wisdom of Feng Shui to the dance floor, and suggest movement techniques based on belly dance to try. I share with you how to tell stories through dance, as well as how to honor the five elements of nature with dance movements. You will also learn about the magic of the costume and how colors bring healing to our lives.

Enjoy!

Rosane

(..over Chicago, January 2004)

Introduction

ENLIGHTENMENT DANCE
How Dance Can Improve the Way You Think, Feel, and Live

THE ANCIENT HISTORY OF DANCE

"The woman of the future will be a free spirit, representing the highest intelligence in the freest body"

- Isadore Duncan

The history of dance is a long one. It has been around as long as we have! Some say that Dance originated in ancient, unknown lands, where people sought a way to perceive their unity with all beings, and merge with the totality of the Universe. Studies have shown that belly dance is the most ancient dance form on the face of Earth.[1] Is it then, the mother of all dances? Is it mere coincidence that Hula Dance from Hawaii, Flamenco from Spain and Samba from Brazil have basic similarities in their movement?

Our ancestors used dance for every aspect of life. They danced to worship. They danced to celebrate the arrival of newborns, to mourn the dead, and every milestone in-between. Dance also played a big part in magic... for example, to attract good fortune, such as rain for the crops, or to dispel bad spirits.

---

[1] See "When The Drummers Were Women" by Lane Redmond, and "The Serpent of The Nile" by Wendy Buonaventura

Sacred dance has always been a form of non-verbal communication between humanity and divinity. Traditional dance movements represent nature and animals in their purest, most divine aspects. The dancers would feel cosmic harmony and merge into a deep state of ecstasy, achieving heightened perception and deeper intuition, and the ability to cope with the trials of their primitive existence: the cold of winter, the darkness of night, storms, floods, the desert winds.

By honoring Nature in all its aspects, and representing them in dance, the ancients developed their inner wisdom. Masks, costumes, jewelry and body painting were used to complement the dance's theme. Over millennia, the specific movements became associated with specific meanings and stories, and thus codified and perpetuated the culture's vital myths.

Much of world mythology is preserved in dance. For example, the Hindus say that Brahma created the art of dance, and gave it as a present to the wizard Bharat, the author of Natya Shastra, the oldest code of dance in the world. Krishna played the flute on a full moon night to seduce the cowgirls to abandon their chores and dance with him. He multiplied himself 16,108 times, partnering with each one of them. This mystical night lasted for six months of our mortal time. Thus it is said that Brahma created dance, but Krishna revealed love through it. And Shiva, known as the *Nataraja* ("dancer"), destroys and re-creates the Universe repeatedly throughout eternity, with the power of his sacred dance!

In Ancient Egypt, rituals in the temple of the Moon Goddess Isis, Goddess of magic and mystery, included dance. Isis represented the feminine aspect of God, and offerings of incense, perfumes, essential oils, flowers and fruits - representing beauty, sensuality and fertility - were made by priestesses who ritually danced their presentation with movements that portrayed animals, gods and nature. Some people theorize that belly dance was originally all about and for women, depicting the very female attributes of sensuality, seduction, sexuality, fertility, conception and labor. The ancient Greeks and Mesopotamians also had very rich dance forms performed by men and women.

ENLIGHTENMENT DANCE
How Dance Can Improve the Way You Think, Feel, and Live

For me, dance is everything. Anyone who can walk can dance, just as anyone who can speak can sing. It is a matter of desire and practice. Today, dance can be a process of self-discovery and creativity. It is a bridge that joins past and future, bringing us inevitably into the present moment, where all miracles occur, and where life really takes place! Let's now explore how dance can enhance your awareness and help you live in the miraculous present moment.

In the next section you are going to learn about this, so new, word of the twenty first century:

Enlightenment

(.. at 35 thousand feet, two hours from San Francisco. November 2003.)

ENLIGHTENMENT THROUGH DANCE

The word enlightenment comes from "Light..." a light that is lit within. Enlightenment for me is an awakening to subtle realities that need to be unveiled by each one of us. I believe we are already enlightened.. we must just let the Light come from within.

One dictionary definition of Enlightenment is "a blessed state in which the individual transcends desire and suffering and attains complete realization." But like most spiritual concepts, the experience transcends definition.

Here are some other attempts at describing enlightenment:*

Nirvana	Knowing Beyond Knowledge
Union / Oneness / Merging	The Peace That Surpasses All Understanding
Deliverance	Self-Liberating Super-Conscious Insight
The Alchemical Transformation.	The Secret Mystery of Life
Original Perfection	The Valuable Essence of All Experience
True Nature	The Absolutely Non-Dependent State
The Eye of Wisdom	Free Awareness
The Light	The Endgame of All Creation
The Goal of the Spiritual Quest	The Living Truth, Unalloyed and Self-Evident

There is a thirst for enlightenment in this new millennium. But in order to understand this newly popular word, we should first understand what it is not.

Today, "religion" is getting old. Many religions' original ideas have fragmented, and they often cause disagreements and even war. Enlightenment is not a religion, though it is the goal, recognized or not, of many religions. Enlightenment is not a belief. Enlightenment is not faith, and it does not need a group to happen! It does not need a

---

* Reprinted with permission from "Enlightenment in Our Time© - The Perennial Wisdom in the New Millennium" by Lonny J. Brown, Ph.D. www.BookLocker.com/lonnybrown

temple or a church. Enlightenment happens within, and it is a deeply personal and unique experience for each individual.

It is in the truth of our actions and in the deepest compassion of our souls that we will find enlightenment. It resides in the silences between our purest thoughts, and in those precious, fleeting moments when we sense eternity. You cannot "seek out" enlightenment, yet it is everywhere you want it to be! In the eyes of an innocent child, in the ecstasy of our feelings when we are in love and in bliss, in that instant before death when your life flashes before your eyes.. Enlightenment is achieved through awareness alone, and appears though our own intention to become more aware. The intent of bringing enlightenment to our lives will make it happen! All we need is a path that can help connect us to that moment. Dance can be one such method.

About three years ago, I read the book "Enlightenment in Our Time," by Lonny Brown, Ph.D. It brought me many insights related to the way I have always experienced my dance! As I digested the enlightening words from this book, I felt in touch with its wisdom, and was uplifted by its inspirations. I corresponded with the author, Dr. Lonny Brown, who is now one of my best friends, and editor of this book. I urge my students and readers to read "Enlightenment in Our Time," because it directly relates to the dance that happens within us: the dance of sorrow, the dance of compassion or the dance of bliss. In this book you will learn how to bring enlightenment to your life. Here is a passage from the book "Enlightenment in our Time":

"It's the perennial wisdom. The ancient knowledge. The Single Truth with ten thousand names. Buried and rediscovered yet again, when the hearts of people yearn for the cessation of their needless anguish.

"The world is shrinking, and the word is out once more, and – you might say – not a moment too soon. In the soul of a whole new generation of seekers and celebrators; in a wave of enlightening teachers from every culture; in the eyes of wise old souls, and highly evolved newborn messengers; in the pure channeled wisdom teachings; in the council circles and sweat lodges.. It's the source of the sacred in every culture and conviction: the timeless Living Spirit emerges and reveals in a new way, on a new day, for a new age: Eclectic. Electronic. Iconoclastic. Trans-cultural. Post-Modern.

Universal. It's time to spiritualize the pulsing global electromagnetic nerve network of our collective intelligence, and realize our essential Godhead. It's time to become enlightened citizens of an enlightened world civilization. And there's no time to waste, for Mankind and the remaining creatures, and the Earth itself are in immanent peril."*

For me, Enlightenment is like being in love!

For me, Enlightenment is a Dance!

Next segment I will invite you to dance enlightenment with me, through

Enlightenment Dance

---

* Note: At the end of Lonny Brown's book are answers to the question, "What is Enlightenment?" from friends and a wide variety ordinary people. This is an on-going public project that you can contribute to. You may also wish to subscribe to Dr. Brown's free monthly e-newsletter, *Enlightenment Online*: Email lonny@holistic.com or visit www.holistic.com/lonny.

WHAT IS ENLIGHTENMENT DANCE?

The Dance of Eternal Bliss

Enlightenment Dance is not to be described but to be experienced. I therefore encourage you to experiment with dance and movement as you read through this book. Enlightenment comes from awareness, and so I created Enlightenment Dance as a series of dance classes designed to promote self-awareness of the body, mind and spirit. The integration of these three is essential: the body is an empty shell, an automaton, without spirit. The spirit is adrift if it cannot feel, and experience through the body. The mind is the essential interpreter between the two, and has no purpose without them.

Enlightenment Dance can be fast or slow; sensual or playful; choreographed or spontaneous; it can be a prayer of the body to reach the deepest levels of the soul, or a celebration of the spirit to enjoy the moments of life. Any dance you do is Enlightenment Dance, if only you intend it to be so, and turn your awareness to that truth!

The movements I use in my classes are influenced by many cultures, particularly those of the Middle East, India and Brazil. I use music from around the world. But Enlightenment Dance is not any one form or fusion of forms. It is an inner exploration of conscious movement and music that uncovers the essence of belly dance, dynamic meditation, yoga, ballet, folk dance, martial arts, tribal celebration.. and much, much more!

Enlightenment Dance bares the feet and the soul, and creatively costumes the body! Above all else, it is fun and joyful! It teaches us to be in the moment, to live life in ecstasy, to appreciate what we have here and now. It is a dance of feeling and healing that captures the magic of being alive. Enlightenment Dance is the Dance of Eternal Bliss!

ENLIGHTENMENT DANCE
How Dance Can Improve the Way You Think, Feel, and Live

THE BENEFITS OF ENLIGHTENMENT DANCING

Enlightenment Dance promotes physical, mental and emotional healing. By enhancing your intimate connection with Spirit, it may increase insights about your well-being, what you are feeling, and life in general. It can help make you more aware of influences in your life and how you react to them.

At the physical level, this dance promotes flexibility, muscular toning, strength and good posture. Enlightenment Dance is not based on the idea of tensing muscles, as in some other western dance forms (such as ballet); it is actually the reverse: you do not have to be tense to be in control. Your body can be relaxed and still be in perfect control of your movement. This lesson can be applied to other aspects of our lives, as well.. just by acknowledging the truth that we do not need to be tense to be in control, but the opposite, very relaxed into the core of our being.

At the emotional level, Enlightenment Dance banishes insecurities, tensions, and emotional blocks, thus promoting creativity, confidence, freedom and sensuality. At the mental level, it develops concentration, mind/body coordination, intuition, and relaxation.

This dance also has a soothing, hypnotic effect on the audience, helping to relax and heal them as well. Healing occurs because the mind steps away from its rationality and allows the spirit to be in the moment where perfection resides. Beholding the dance, the audience is captivated to share the bliss of the dancer. There is a communion of energy and spiritual bounding that emerges in a kindred way throughout the performance.

The movements are performed in isolation, with parts of the body moving independently. It involves geometric shapes, such as spirals, infinity signs, and circles. These shapes are related to nature symbolism and subconscious archetypes that connect us to our humanity and divinity, and promote a sense of unity between dancer and audience.

This is because all these forms are infused in nature, in our bodies, and in the heavenly bodies. You can see them in turtle shells, spider webs, snakes, trees, the cells in our bodies, on our finger prints, and in the galaxies! We are part of all these nature aspects, and dancing the symbolism awakes this relationship with nature.. mostly forgotten in our modern life. This dance promotes a feeling of unity, of eternity and of belonging, something that we all long for.

So dance to your heart's content! It not only feels good, and is therapeutic, but your audience will feel the healing as well!

Next chapter, I would like to start by sharing with you about moving meditation, a way to dive beyond self to achieve all knowingness.

(Crew Operations Lounge, Dallas Fort Worth, October 2003)

Enlightening the Mind

ENLIGHTENMENT DANCE MEDITATION

"What is Dance?"

by Adnan Sarhan

> *A real and true dance creates communication with the people who are watching, and with the drum you become a moving rhythm. Your spirit takes over the body and tells the body what to do. When the spirit commands the body, the body will become an instrument of marvels. The body projects itself in exaltation and elation, and the cosmic energy opens itself and flows to the body and energizes the body with vitality, beauty and intelligence. The dancing is the yearning of the spirit for freedom. The body dances to the rhythm of the spirit when the rhythm of the spirit and the perfected rhythm of the drum join together. The dance becomes the life of the moment. When you are in the moment, the moment expands and becomes a tranquil sea of time. The spiritual pleasure becomes the essence of the sea of time. To go to the spirit, you will get the spirit. You will fall in love with the spirit and the spirit exposes itself to you. The spirit is love, joy, pleasure and delight and it is the life. Spirit is not a lecture or strict behavior of didactic imposition or solemn rigidity. It is only when the people don't know what the spirit is or where spirit is or pretend they are spirit, then they become stiff, contracted, and catalepsy is the extreme opposition of spirit. When the dance becomes perfected, deep and real, it becomes a living dance that makes the life within more alive, more aware, more intelligent, more alert and awake in the moment. True and real dance is never in the past or the future. It is in the present and the present becomes the heaven of dance. The dance brings transcendence to a higher reality and the dance becomes a song dancing with the stars. The mist becomes the veil of the dancer. The dancing song and the undulating veil sway with the breeze. The night of Scheherazade becomes alive and the echo of the lute penetrates the heart of night. The spirit becomes the dance and the dance becomes the spirit and the life becomes lovable. The moment of the lovable life becomes fragrant with the perfume of heaven, and life becomes contentment and the pleasure of spirit becomes its depth. Dancing brings lively energy to the place and charm to the people.*

When the dance is perfected and it comes from the depth of the mind, the body, the feeling, the emotion and the spirit, the dance becomes magical, phenomenal, delightful experience.

The body becomes an instrument of cosmic energies with the force of life and invokes transcending aspiration. The moment becomes life, love joy and pleasure that come from the spirit and transcend the mundane senses to senses that are bathed with the attribute of spirit. The time flows and unfolds and the dance becomes a phenomenon of evolution to perfection and makes life blend in a union with the creation.[2]

---

[2] Adnan Sarhan, Sufi master and drummer, born in Baghdad, travels the world giving workshops and performing drum and dance concerts. He has trained many people to become great dancers and teachers. His commitment to his work is evident in the effectiveness and joy of his workshops. He lives what he teaches, giving a profound experience of what he calls the spirit. In the summer he holds a three month intensive in the mountains of New Mexico where the pure air and gentle forests support the healing process that takes place.

WHAT IS DANCE MEDITATION?

In meditative dance, we use movement with breath to achieve a more relaxed and aware state of mind. This calms the busy mind and eliminates distracting thoughts, particularly when we are stressed and under pressure. Such "moving meditation" can create feelings of ecstasy and bliss, promoting a sense of being fully alive in the moment.

In class, there is minimal verbal instruction. This process allows the perceptions of our senses to blossom. Through improvisation, we develop fluidity and connection to the self, the music, and the moment. This style of following simple movements as they change and build momentum relaxes the mind and releases tension. It opens up creativity and brings awareness to the feelings of the music and the movement. Thus, the self, the music, and the movement are connected in the moment.

Allow your breath to be your guide. Gabrielle Roth, in her book <u>Sweat Your Prayers</u>, says *"most people don't breathe below the neck. Yoga exercises aim at controlling breath. I want to set the breath free and release all the pent-up energies in the body that keep it from moving."*

Exhale and inhale with awareness - for each step, a breath; for each gesture, another breath. Each movement guides the next, like an endless motion of energy, gathered inwards. The mind travels freely in the enjoyment of the timeless now. Thoughts evaporate when the body is the guide. This exhilarating experience is a conscious process of surrender to the music. *Let your breath be your guide.* There's no right or wrong… all movement is spontaneous, vivid and complete!

Moving Meditation can be a metaphor for life. Sometimes it is necessary to move straight ahead; other times it is better to back off, sidestep, or move in a circle, until you sense a way out. When you meditate you achieve wholeness, you access the unity that surrounds all that is alive on the planet. You dive beyond self to achieve all-knowingness.

Stillness meditation might be hard for some. Living in big cities surrounded by traffic jams and background noise can make it quite impossible to still the mind. Paradoxically, I found out that I can only still my mind if I move my body!

Want to give it a try?

(..at the Holiday Inn, London - 6 hours ahead of my home time.)

DANCE MEDITATION EXERCISE

Set the intent of freeing your body. Relax your mind by just stating to yourself:

"My mind and my body are free and present to enjoy the benefits of this dance meditation exercise"

- Choose a slow, flowing song that you love.

- Standing barefoot, close your eyes as you begin breathing slowly and deep, bringing your awareness to your body,

- Bring your attention to your feet, and move them slowly, from side to side.

- As you shift your weight from one side to the other, inhale and exhale accordingly.

- Become aware of your knees and feel how they are connected to your legs and feet. Keep shifting your weight from side to side. Inhale to the right and exhale to the left keep it steady... for every movement, a breath.

- Next, attend to your hips, and move them from side to side... follow the music... feel how your feet, knees and hips are connected.

- Open your eyes slightly, gently gazing at the objects you see.

- Let your hips lead the movement, by just placing your attention on them.

- Move out of the spot, go forward, go back, and travel sideways.

- Open your arms and let them flow along with your hips.

- Think about how your arms can guide your dance and let them show you where to go.

- Bring awareness to the relation of the arms to the hips and let them dance together.

- Allow your arms to rise up, and then settle down.

- Follow the music.

- Synchronize your breath to each movement.

- Inhale and bring your arm up. Exhale and bring your arm down.

- As you begin to glide through the space, bring your attention to your shoulders and head and feel how they are connected.

- Move your head and move your shoulders through the music. Breathe!

- Follow the music with your whole body by letting your limbs dance.

- Scan with your awareness from top down to your feet, becoming aware of each area in turn.

- As the music comes to a close, sit down on the floor and stay there for a moment, sensing the inner dance that still goes on within your body.

- Allow your thoughts to flow, with the intention of just letting them go. Bring your attention to all the physical sensations: the temperature of your skin, the rhythm of your heart, the taste in your mouth, the odors of your surroundings, and the sound of the silence.

(NYC- JFK airport lounge, waiting for flight 64 to Zurich, May 2003.)

ENLIGHTENMENT DANCE
How Dance Can Improve the Way You Think, Feel, and Live

AWARENESS & INTENT
Developing Awareness and Bringing Intent to your Dance

Intention is the core of all conscious life. It is our intentions that create karma, our intentions that help others, our intentions that lead us away from the delusions of individuality toward the immutable verities of enlightened awareness. Conscious intention colors and moves everything.

- Master Hsing Yun, "Describing the Indescribable"

Typically, in our social training process, the focus is on the outside, physical world. We are more concerned with how we look then how we feel. We live life mandated by social expectations that don't often reflect how we really are. Society trains us not to be the true originators of our thoughts, but to follow those that already exist.

We imagine that this is how things inherently are, rather than discovering that this is only one way to perceive reality. But life does not have to be led according to pre-assigned beliefs. *We can create an entirely new course for ourselves (and for society) by changing our intentions.*

To achieve peace, we need to be aware of the intentions we are using in each and every moment of our life... and this can only be accomplished by a watchful perception of the thoughts and beliefs behind our decisions and choices. Perceive your thoughts by asking yourself questions: *Why do I believe this? Why did I choose to say that? What makes me act this way?* This process allows us to get to know more who we are. Conversely, when we are not focused on our intent we truly are not centered in ourselves.

We need to question the idea of "success." It must be perceived at the level of self-realization instead of social status. Only when you are authentically happy with your activities, will you truly make a creative difference and transform your life (and the world) for the better.

Because my two vocations seem so different, people ask me, *how can you be a Flight Attendant and a professional dance teacher at the same time?* My answer is that I love both! If someone happened to ask me if I would fly to Paris with 270 people, spend a night and a day there and return, I would do it for free! If someone asks me to teach the Samba, I would start immediately, and he or she would have a crash course in Brazilian dance on the spot, for free. But they pay me for that too!

Flying has brought me so many opportunities for my dance career! I have learned from show business veterans in New York, and taught classes during stopovers in Sao Paulo. As a Flight Attendant, I can travel to England for free, and as a Dance Instructor, I can work with my students on the Isle of Wight when I get there! Find out what *you* love to do! The true test is to ask, *would I do this for free?*

Ask yourself what is the intent behind what you do. If the answer gives you a good feeling, you will know you are in the right track. If the answer makes you insecure, keep asking yourself again and again, until you find an answer that will totally make sense to you.

I truly believe that intention and awareness are the keys to evolution, both personal and planetary. We can bring our highest intent to our lives by simply paying attention. In the next section, you'll learn how to practice this through dance.

🕊 (..in a 767 jumbo jet galley flying from Paris to New York, March 2004.)

PAYING ATTENTION, USING INTENT

Attention is concentration and observation.

When we give attention to something we make it grow, whether it is something good, like our children, or bad, like our worries. If you have a problem and start to think about it a lot, it gets bigger. In the same way, when something wonderful happens to you, and you give attention to it, you feel even happier! Most of the time we are not aware of the attention we give to certain things and our intent to be happy is somehow lost in our busy mind. We allow ourselves to drift through life's experiences like a dream, without awareness and without perception. It is like sailing a boat without a compass.

The more attention we give to our dance movements, the more in-tune with our feelings we are, and the more vivid and real our expression.

Sometimes my dance students get so focused on whether their body is moving right that they lose track of their feelings. This is because Western education is based on copying and comparing. We feel afraid of being judged "wrong" if we don't follow pre-established patterns. Fearing rejection, we accept *copying* instead of *learning*. We forget that we are individuals, and grow up following rules and learning to be who we aren't.

So, we must open up to real creativity. First, remember that we are all different from each other and that our dance will reflect those differences. There's no right no wrong; there is just the dance. Of course it is useful to study choreographs because it helps to improve our movement vocabulary, but it is imperative that we go beyond the sameness to discover and re-invent ourselves in a brand new way!

TIP: Learn the movements of a choreography first and then, after they get into your muscle memory, let the emotions flow by not thinking about the movement anymore, but tuning up to your body's sensation.

<u>Intention</u> is the thought <u>behind</u> the attention that we give to something. For example, my attention right now is on writing this book. My intent is to share with my students and readers my personal experience and insights of what Enlightenment Dance is about, and to leave a gift to the world.

It is the intention that feeds the attention, even if it is unconscious. Intentions can create or destroy. When you bring intention, and thus, attention to your movements, it can manifest powerful changes within you.

"Energy flows where attention goes," my friend and dance teacher, Janeeda used to say. By paying attention to physical sensations and how they affect our feelings, we develop strong awareness of our emotions. We can then learn to direct energy constructively, and not disperse it with unpleasant, destructive thoughts. We can consciously guide the process of emotional release.

For instance, I find myself in an argument with a friend. The argument leads us to make comments that hurt our feelings. So, instead of directing my attention to the argument and continuing it, I *pay attention* and focus on the effect that this is producing in my body: I notice that my throat is tighter and my heart is pounding. I observe how this affects my body and I understand that these are symptoms of the argument. By being consciously aware of this process, I fully understand the situation, and place the <u>intent</u> of being at peace with my friend by finding ways to diffuse the argument. (It is better to lose the argument than to lose a friend, isn't it?). Pretty soon the feeling of emotional turmoil is transmuted. By directing my <u>attention</u> to the solution, instead of "feeding" the hostile energy, I release it from my body, consciously breathing it out.

Or, I may choose to discuss the argument a little more, with the <u>intention</u> to get through to my friend. If the emotion is too intense, and I feel like crying, I let myself do it. Crying releases energy and it is a very honest way of healing. It is important to not keep the emotion locked inside. Emotion needs to flow. If it doesn't flow it stagnates in the body and pushes your mind to obsess over the same issue over and over again. This drags you down and feeds the energy that is causing the argument, even though you might not be aware of it.

If the argument resolution scenario that I have suggested doesn't work out, it may be necessary to leave, to avoid hostility. Take time to understand and release inner emotions. Such arguments might have triggered emotions from the past that may need time to be released. Do so with your <u>intent</u>. Let the intent take care of the emotion. Let your breath be your guide in all circumstance of your life!

Dance gives an immediate experience of the feedback flow of energy because it is a physical act that has no other purpose but to express our emotion creatively. Dance, like music, occurs only in the present moment, beat by beat. *It is nearly impossible to dance and not be present!* Dance automatically attunes body and mind, which can then set the intent. Usually, intent is set unconsciously. *Just by becoming aware of having fun, we set the intent of joy!*

Thoughts have form. They also release energy. When thoughts are carried by the breath through speech, they manifest into reality, and are multiplied in the minds of everyone who hears or reads them. Do you wonder why there are so many negative circumstances in the world? Could it be the prevalence of our imbalanced, unhappy thoughts, and the attention we give them? Dance can help you to tune your thoughts to joy, just like changing the TV channel from 24-hour war coverage to something a bit more uplifting.

When energy is released with intent, it has the power to make things happen, as when we think of someone just before they call on the phone. This kind of synchronicity happens on the unconscious level.

If we bring awareness to our actions, and direct the flow of energy by putting our intent into that attention, we can manifest powerful, magical "coincidences" that are not really coincidences, but a true realization of our intent (whether conscious or unconscious).

For example, I want to buy a new costume (intention). I consciously bring to my mind exactly how it looks: color, size, style… (attention). I dance and release the energy I am producing with my movements with that specific intent. Releasing means not to be concerned anymore. Once you release, don't bring it back to your thoughts; just completely let go. This is when magic happens. It is a form of trusting that the universe will fulfill your request.

Practice developing this "manifestation" awareness when you dance. First, take a few moments before you start to move to set the <u>intention</u> of your dance. Then, allow your <u>attention</u> to focus on the physical sensation of your movement, letting the energy of each movement flow naturally to the next. By being consciously aware of the energy flow without trying to control your movement or impose logic on it, you will experience the best results.

Learning how to apply awareness and intent to your dance helps you do the same in other areas of your life. You will develop awareness of your thoughts and emotions, and learn to place your intent to "feed" only those that promote well-being and happiness. That is why *dance is a tool for enlightenment and empowerment.* Enlightenment Dance can bring us into the ecstatic feeling of being fully alive in the eternal present. It is a great adventure, and you are the guide! This is the dance of eternal bliss!

Remember as you do the following exercise that *the greatest benefits of dance come from awareness, awareness comes from attention, and attention comes from intention.*

DANCE INTENTION & AWARENESS EXERCISE

- Set your intent – what do you want? Which kind of changes do you need for your life?

- Choose music that touches you deeply.

- Begin by moving your limbs in isolation.

- Be aware of your body sensations.

- Focus on each body part, and feel how it wants to move (follow the dance meditation exercise on page 19 •).

- With your breath, visualize your intent.

- Make it clear in your mind. If it is an object, visualize it in detail: color, size, shape. If it is an accomplishment or an event, think about what, who, when, why, how.. The more details you put into it, the more powerful the manifestation will be.

- Finish your dance and release your intent.. no more thinking about it!

Now that your intent is getting clear, let's move on to the dance behind your thoughts.

(..flying to Brazil, July 2003)

THE ENLIGHTENMENT DANCE OF THOUGHTS

The breath feeds the soul and the breath will take you to heaven. The breath feeds the ego and the breath will take you to hell. It is the thought that is carried on the breath which determines your very rise or fall. If your thought is positive, you will be positive, and if it is negative, you will be negative.

If you project in your mind a perfumed rose, with breath to animate the rose in your imagination, you will mentally create an image of a sweet garden. That garden and the sweetness of the rose will help to elevate you to tranquility. Tranquility will help you to be peaceful.

Your thoughts will be peaceful thoughts and you will be in a state of peace. Scatteredness, tension and negativity will disappear. Serenity, pleasant feelings and a mood of delight will become the normal way of life if you wish it to be that way.

- Adnan Sarhan

In the last chapter, I described thoughts as having form and being energy. We carry thoughts in our mind all the time. It is a challenge to empty the mind and enjoy the bliss of just being in the moment. It would be wonderful to be able to feel enlightened all the time and live a joyful life.

How do we do that? How can we have control of our thoughts, or achieve that state of mind seekers call enlightenment? Well, the Yogis say that there are four kinds of thoughts that travel through our minds: positive, negative, useful and non-useful.

<u>Positive</u> thoughts are those of admiration, love, friendship and compassion: *I admire Lonny Brown. I enjoy my friend Janet's company. I truly wish to understand what you are feeling.* <u>Useful</u> thoughts are those that have utility: *"I will clean the house today." "I will make spinach lasagna for dinner tonight." "I want to call Christine about tomorrow's rehearsal." "I have to miss my doctor's appointment because I am busy with school work."* (Even though it is a "problem" this thought has "utility"). *"I am upset with my boss because he did not give me the raise, but I will talk to him tomorrow."*

It is said that if we could keep only positive and useful thoughts in our mind, we would be filled up with life force/energy, and never feel sick or sad. When this does happen, energy flows freely throughout the body, and you are so invigorated that you have more than enough energy to share with others. On the other hand, negative thoughts tend to create feelings of anger, jealousy or fear: *"I hate when you're late." "I think you are more beautiful than me." "I'm not good enough for this job." "I'll never forgive you. "*

<u>Non-useful</u> thoughts are the opposite of useful ones, those that reflect blame or a condition,, an event you feel guilty about or something you wish that hasn't happened. These kind of thoughts are based on something that you can no longer change. Non-useful thinking stifles skillful action. Such thoughts usually start with "if" or "when:" *"If only I were rich, I'd be happy." "When I buy my house, then I'll be happier." "When I finish school I'll really be happy!" "If he didn't hurt me, I would love him." "Only when my kids grow up will I be really free."* Such thought patterns state a condition for good feelings,

but prevent you from feeling good at the present moment. Blame is useless, because it doesn't solve the problem. Guilt is only self blame, and is equally useless. Problems are only fixed when someone takes responsibility and acts.

<u>Negative</u> and <u>non-useful</u> thoughts can drain the life force right out of your body, like a bucket with a hole. It flows out, leaving you feeling tired, even when you've done nothing strenuous. When our negative and counter-productive thoughts persist, our health deteriorates. The mental habit of negativity snowballs: Because we feel sick, we have more negative and non-useful thoughts, and because we have more non-useful and negative thoughts, we feel sicker.. it is a useless cycle of self-pity, worry, and fear.

If you create a habit of watching your thoughts, you can control them. Make this your intention when dancing. Dance automatically brings your thoughts into the present moment, so watch what thoughts surface as you dance, and what emotions those thoughts make you feel. Then you can *intentionally transform the negative and non-useful thoughts and emotions through the movement of your body*.

Next, I will show you a powerful Moving Meditation technique that will rapidly put you in an enlightened state of mind.

Give this a try!

THOUGHTS TRANSMUTATION DANCE EXERCISE

- Start your dance (follow the Dance Meditation exercise instructions on page 19 •).

- Pay attention to the thoughts that come to your mind, always remembering to focus on your breath.

- Define each thought as it appears in your mind: Is it positive? Negative? Is it useful or non-useful?

- Transmute negative thoughts by rethinking them positively (ex: replace *"I don't like my body"* with *"I am so happy my body is perfect and allows me to move and to dance."*)

- Transmute non-useful thoughts (ex: *"If I were skinnier I would dance better"* becomes *"I am learning to appreciate and love my body as it is."*)

- Repeat and reinforce all the positive and useful thoughts. (ex: *"This kind of dance would be fascinating with my new sky blue costume! - Yes! I will look like a Goddess!"* or *"I love this music, it makes me feel heavenly! I can't wait to perform this dance on-stage!"*

If other, life-issue type thoughts appear, do the same. Place the intent of carrying this thought control pattern into your daily life. You will be able to enjoy all the benefits of it!

TIP: Transcend negative thinking with this affirmation: *The more I dance, the more I transmute and elevate thoughts. The more positive thoughts I have, the better I feel. The better I feel the more I want to dance!*

(Crew Operations Lounge at JFK, NYC, Dec 2003)

ENLIGHTENMENT DANCE
How Dance Can Improve the Way You Think, Feel, and Live

SENSATIONS & FEELING & EMOTIONS
Transmuting Sensations & Feelings by Dancing your Emotions

SENSATION (sèn-sâ´shen) noun: *(body)*

1.a. *A perception associated with stimulation of a sense organ or with a specific body condition: the sensation of heat; a visual sensation.*

   b. *The faculty to feel or perceive; physical sensibility.*

   c. *An indefinite, generalized body feeling: a sensation of lightness.*

2. *A state of heightened interest or emotion: "The anticipation produced in me a sensation somewhat between bliss and fear"* (James Weldon Johnson).*

FEELING (feeling) noun:\ *(mind)*

An awareness or impression. A general impression conveyed by a person, place, or thing. a. Appreciative regard or understanding. b. Intuitive awareness or aptitude; a feel.

EMOTION (î-mo´shen) noun: *(spirit)*

   1. *An intense mental state that arises subjectively rather than through conscious effort and is often accompanied by physiological changes; <u>a strong feeling</u>: the emotions of joy, sorrow, reverence, hate, and love.*

   2. *A state of mental agitation or disturbance.*

   3. *The part of the consciousness that involves <u>feeling</u>; <u>sensibility</u>.*

Sensation, feeling, and emotion correspond to the body, mind and soul. I like to compare this to the spiritual trilogy of the father, the son and the Holy Spirit which can be experienced in the body; not just as a mental belief.

---

* Bliss and fear are emotions. The tingling they can both produce is a sensation. Excitement is an emotion. The physical rush it produces is a sensation.

You can train your body to be sensitive to the different energies that circulate in your life, assimilating what is desirable and dissipating what is not, by dancing or moving with **awareness**. It is an inner sense of connectedness with sensations, feelings, and emotions.

For each emotion we experience, a sensation and a feeling preceded it. For example, you meet a person and you have a "feeling" that you know her. Then you have the "sensation" of familiarity and comfort, or nostalgia, recalled by memories of the two of you together in elementary school. You hug your friend, expressing your "emotion" of love, and happiness to see her.

Sensations, feelings and emotions interplay constantly in dance, as in life. It is by bringing awareness to this process that we can learn to transmute negative emotions into blissful ones. Our emotions touch others, just as we are touched by other's emotions throughout our lives.

From our very earliest days, emotions are a vital part of our experience of reality. When you understand this process and allow yourself to be aware of the intersection between sensations, feelings and emotions, you access a creative healing power. As each one of us heals emotionally from our past, we free ourselves to feel joy and unconditional love. This can happen through dance. By dancing our emotions, we get in touch with who we truly are. We resonate with and reflect our humanity and our soul becomes visible to the audience.

Note: these terms are interchangeable. A sensation is physical, like pain, or a tickle, or tingling… but you can also "sense" something, like a sixth "sense," or like the definition of "feeling;" e.g., "I get a feeling there is something wrong here," is synonymous with "I sense something is wrong here," or "I get the feeling (or I sense) you are upset with me." But "feeling" can also be synonymous with "emotion," like "you hurt my feelings!" "I'm feeling sad," or it can be a sensation, too, like "I don't feel well, I feel sick… I feel dizzy… I feel tired." Often the thought (mental) "I feel like something is wrong" is hard to distinguish from the underlying feeling/emotion (spirit) of fear, because the physical, underlying sensations that define fear (rapid heartbeat, heart in throat, stomach flutter) happen almost simultaneously/instantaneously with the thought and the emotion.

Dance, like dreaming, unveils many levels of our subconscious, and our universal essence. When we dance with this perspective, we can transcend fears, sadness or anger and be transported -- through the experience of the sensations, feelings, and emotions -- to a more vivid and aware state. We can thus truly integrate body, mind, and spirit in an adventurous transformation towards enlightenment.

Regardless of the terms used, it is important to embrace rather than avoid feelings (emotions); they come to heal the traumas of your life. Emotions need to be fully experienced, to flow through the body and be released. Just as we express and release happy emotions, we need to learn to experience and let go of the sad ones. Nobody laughs about a joke continuously for years. Why then do we tend to hold on to fear, sadness and anger? Emotions, if not felt freely, are bottled up, but they never really go away – they fester until they resurface, worse than before. Let them go, just like the last joke!

There are times in our lives that we experience a lot of problems and pain. It seems that life is constantly playing emotional roller coaster with us! So, after we fall, we must learn how to get up again. I feel pain because I am going through a divorce. The pain seems to grow if I feed it with victimized feelings such as *"poor me, how come this happened to me? I am so lost now, what to do? I am so sad and upset because of this and that.."*

Instead, I focus on the present moment and on finding out ways to transmute my feelings. Just by not taking things too seriously and by focusing on the benefits of starting a new single life, I feel better. I release my pain, by thinking about how can I make the most of this situation, and how I can bring my attention to the present moment. So, even though I feel like crawling into a hole, I force myself to stand up by initially "faking it" with a striking idea. For example, one thing I found that works for me is to use red lipstick and high-heels! They are wonderful for raising my self-esteem by improving my body posture and making me feel more attractive. As I receive more attention, I intend to use this attention as a healing mechanism to switch my "depressed" mode into an "uplifted" one. I find out that the "sad" feeling is lost like the last joke I laughed about and forgot.

Of course this process of reversing emotions is not always easy. We are surrounded by people who unconsciously support our neuroses and pains. It seems that our unhappiness is almost encouraged, if only because it resonates with the weaknesses of so many others. So many seem to have lost their essence and to have become out of touch with their true Self.

Who are we? What are we here for? If you stop and close your eyes for a moment you can remember that you are not here to be unhappy. You must find happiness within yourself, apart from any circumstance and any person in this world. To be in the moment is one key. Another is to learn to play, to open up the mind for creativity, and not take the problems that appear in our lives too seriously.

Most of our "problems" are illusory. We don't realize how we create them unwittingly. Even with tragic life episodes such as sickness and death, I suggest trying to find peace by tuning into the moment, in the breath. Let the feeling of sorrow come and go, like everything else. It might take days or weeks, but the best strategy is to continually release it, instead of just accepting, indulging and feeding the sorrow. Ultimately, the best choice is happiness. If you are happy you are contributing to a better world. It is as if we are all part of a big engine, with some broken parts. If you "fix yourself," you will be one less broken piece in the universe. So, please help us all by helping yourself!

Now let's learn how to do an emotional release exercise through dance.

EMOTIONAL RELEASE DANCE EXERCISE

Dance can be emotionally healing when we allow painful feelings that arise to be felt and accepted with love and patience. This can become quite creative by fully expressing these feelings exactly how they "want" to come through and be released.

- ❂ Choose a song or music that you love and that touches you deeply.

- ❂ Acknowledge any memories that arise of painful events or old wounds. Pay particular attention to how your body feels as you recall the episode.

- ❂ Trust your body. Move limbs freely and intuitively.

- ❂ Breathe with your movements: inhale with each expansion, exhale with each contraction.

- Recall as much detail of the remembered incident as possible.

- Feel your emotions and "gut" feelings as you felt them in the past, and now, in reaction to this exercise; dance them.

- Your memory will bring insights and desires.* For example, a new idea can come to mind of something that you have never thought about, or a wish can pop up and ignite your passion.

- Follow these intuitive changes. When you have a desire to correct something, or if there is something you wish you could have said or asked, do so in your imagination.

- Keep dancing... keep breathing. Give your emotions expression: cry your tears, shout or stomp your anger, curl up around your pain and surrender it. It is only by thus accepting and releasing these emotions that you can transmute them. In other words, give them free reign to express themselves fully and completely, and experience their full force. It may sound paradoxical, but completely feeling these negative states is the first step to transcending them.

- Dance with your whole body: elbows, hands, shoulders, hips, legs, feet, spine, neck. Move the energy throughout your body.

- Move in different directions, shifting your weight and direction.

- Move your eyes from right to left, back and forth, slow and fast - as in REM (rapid eye movement) sleep. This shifts the energy from one brain hemisphere to the other, in order to process the emotions on all levels in all brainwave* patterns.

- Stay with this process, dancing and reliving the memory over and over from beginning to end, like a movie, until you feel all

---

* "Insight" is the ability to look at a situation and apprehend what is happening from the information available.
* Brain waves are an electrical representation of neural synaptic activity. They can indicate the regions of the brain that are active as well as the intensity of the activity. The instrument used to display these waves is the electroencephalograph.

the feelings, imagine all the alternative "happy endings," and "rewrite" the memory completely through the healing images that come up naturally.

- When you have reached a final healing image (have a feeling of finality), imagine merging this image into the original wounded picture of your actual memory. Feel carefully what happens when these two images are merged.

Remember: *Let your body dance with the joy of the divine in each present moment! Dance with feeling! Dance and feel the sensations! Dance transmuting your emotions! Embrace the bliss! Your dance is becoming your enlightened guru. Embrace it with ecstasy!*

(.. on-board a 777 jumbo jetliner, flying over the Amazon forest, August 2003)

ENLIGHTENMENT DANCE
How Dance Can Improve the Way You Think, Feel, and Live

ECSTATIC DANCING

"To Dance then, is to pray, to meditate, to enter into communion with the larger dance, which is the universe."

- Jean Houston

Ecstatic dance is a formless sacred expression of the body in rhythm. It is moving prayer. It frees the spirit to achieve a sensitive state of awareness, through which a powerful creative process occurs.

Many civilizations of the past, and indigenous cultures even today, use the power of ecstatic dance to travel between the material and spiritual worlds, and journey into the deeper realms of the psyche. They know how to invite the life force to heal the dancer. Our modern world seems to isolate us from this energy, which is nature's essence. Ecstatic dance allows us to re-embody this wisdom, like recovering lost parts of ourselves.

There are no right or wrong steps in ecstatic dance. All you need do is to relax, surrender into the rhythms, and let your spirit be the guide.

This type of dance is holistic in that it synchronizes left and right brain hemispheric functioning. Following an ecstatic dance experience, you will usually feel more refreshed and alert than when you began. A sense of euphoria and bliss will take over your soul when you dance ecstatically, as you unlock subconscious doors in the psyche. This can be described as a visionary experience of a mystical or spiritual nature.

In these dance experiences, people may communicate with spirit guides, animal or nature spirits, the earth, or sacred symbols, or find themselves immersed in what is described as a divine healing light or energy. A profound sense of unity with one's self, humanity, nature, the cosmos, and a greater source of being often accompanies these experiences.

ECSTATIC DANCE EXPERIENCE

I recommend dancing with the sounds of nature as often as possible. Dance under the moon, with bugs singing, the wind rustling the leaves, the birds calling and the magical sound of flowing waters for your music!

Scientists say that bright artificial light inhibits the production of melatonin, which is also associated with rejuvenation, relaxation and deep, restful sleep. When dancing at home, keep the lights natural or low. At night, when we see by starlight, moonlight, candlelight or firelight, the brain produces melatonin, a key hormone related to religious and euphoric states. The flickering of a fire burning in the middle of the circle also makes the optic nerve stimulate the pineal, pituitary, and hypothalamus.

Dancing alone is as profound as dancing in a group. Both are equally powerful. When dancing in a group, encourage everyone to participate, including children and seniors. Those who are disabled can dance in whatever way they can, even if it is only by tapping a finger or swaying their heads. Group dancing in a circle is quite wonderful.

Dance steps and body movements are unique for each person, as they find their own alignment with universal rhythms. Let the movement flow and carry you away! Dancing with eyes closed much of the time is helpful to some people in order to be uninhibited and maintain inner focus. *Become the dance!*

If you have a chance to create an enclosed space for ecstatic dancing, make it round with a dome or pyramid roof with a skylight to let in the natural moonlight. Use natural earth, stone or wood for floors, or natural fiber rugs. Make the environment beautiful and conducive to higher states with art, symbols, gently billowing cloths, and plants.

If you are dancing in a square or rectangular space, transform it into a circle as much as possible with curtains, pillows, screens, furniture, or plants, or do it in your imagination. The circle focuses healing and spiritual energies.

Powerful ecstatic emotions of gratitude and happiness generated during the dance strongly attract positive conditions: feelings of grace, a sense of accomplishment, ease, security, satisfaction and happiness.

In any place, at any time, it is possible to create in your imagination the seashore with its crashing surf, calling birds and blissful wind. Or transport yourself into a deep forest with chirping insects, hooting owls, and laughing rivers; or a mystical cave overlooking the desert with flickering firelight; or a beautiful spherical temple filled with power objects and symbols of divine perfection. Imagine your dance!

Experiment, dancing and focusing on one sense at a time. Dance blindfolded and then dance with wide eyes open; dance tasting a cinnamon stick or a chocolate candy; dance smelling incense burning or a cake baking; dance hearing the music very high and then very low; dance touching yourself or things around you. Dance fast to slow songs and slow for fast songs! Improvise. You will be amazed at your discoveries!

(..just before landing in Guatemala, January 2004.)

Enlightening the Soul

ENLIGHTENMENT DANCE
How Dance Can Improve the Way You Think, Feel, and Live

OPENING THE CHAKRAS THROUGH DANCE

CHAKRAS - YOUR PSYCHIC ENERGY CENTERS

by Lonny J. Brown PhD.

There is an ancient treasure map to the highest states of consciousness located as close as your own spinal column. Seven major landmarks along the way - called chakras - correspond to the stages of human development through which we all eventually pass. When all our centers are "open," we realize our full potential.

Wheels of Power

If you are alive, you are "wired" and charged with energy. Within you is a vast network of nerves which conduct electrical impulses between the central nervous system and the muscles, organs, glands, and sensory receptors throughout the body.

Our bodies are comprised of countless numbers of cells, each holding a critical chemical balance of conductive minerals, insulating proteins, and electrolytic salts; each a potential receiver of these minute electro-chemical currents. In effect, every cell is a miniature living power plant, and several trillion of them, aligned and in circuit, generate the bio-electromagnetic field in which - and by which - you live and move. This life-energy is called "prana," in India, and "chi" in China. Mapping this internal circuitry, the Chinese evolved the healing art of acupuncture, which stimulates energy flow along "meridians."

The full three-dimensional "field effect" of all your energy is sometimes referred to as the "etheric body" or "aura." This highly active force field both reflects your state of health and responds to stimulation - a finding of some significance in medicine. It is a property of all living organisms, and is detectable with sensitive magnetometers, infra-red sensors, Kirlian photography, and other field scanning devices. This energy is both the creative force and vital sustainer of the physical body, and connects it with mind and emotions.

The Sanskrit word "chakra" means "wheel." The chakras within the human energy field are vortices of life force, where it concentrates like sunlight through a lens. Chakras are located in various places within the body, including the palms and the soles of the feet, but the seven most significant occur along the length of the spine. They are depicted in the medical symbol, the Caduceus, as the crossing points of two rising snakes, the positive and negative energy currents. These energy foci are not anatomical structures, though they do correspond to various endocrine glands.

The "yoga" or "internal science" of opening the energy centers has endured for five thousand years, because it works! Chakra meditation is experience-based, not theoretical or magical. With specific, systematic mental practices, you can induce or accelerate functional improvements in various organs and glands, as well as positive, psycho-spiritual growth.

Aside from their organic relevance, each chakra represents a psychologically different way of perceiving reality, and interacting with the world. One can think of the chakras as "sub-personalities," or stages of development. Furthermore, human evolution itself embodies our progression through these stages, from primal to Divine.

Through careful application of core relaxation techniques, breath awareness exercises, imagery, and intonation, an inner stream of concentrated energy is released upwards through the central channel of the spine. Thus, the seven chakras can be conceived as psychic valves - though they cannot be forcibly opened. (They are also frequently depicted as flowers).[3]

---

[3] Reprinted with permission from "Enlightenment in Our Time© - The Perennial Wisdom in the New Millennium" by Lonny J. Brown, Ph.D. www.BookLocker.com/lonnybrown To order "Journey Through The Chakras" audio tape, a guided meditation and visualization with. Lonny J. Brown, Ph.D., go to www.holistic.com/lonny

ENLIGHTENMENT DANCE
How Dance Can Improve the Way You Think, Feel, and Live

THE CHAKRAS: SUBTLE and PHYSICAL CONNECTIONS

1st: The Root Chakra

Located at the base of the spine - related to survival, security and the will to live. A blocked first chakra can make you unaware of your own needs and keep you caught up in the struggle to survive. An open first chakra gives you a firm sense of who you are and helps you transcend your fears. The color is red.

2nd: The Pleasure Chakra

About four inches bellow the navel - related to sex and procreation but also symbolizes creativity in general, A blocked 2nd chakra may cause struggles with sexuality and creativity, which often leads to compulsive behavior. An open 2nd chakra creates comfort with sexuality and creativity - and helps you break out of old patterns where your energy feels blocked. The color is orange.

3rd: Center Chakra "Solar Plexus"

Located in the digestive system, this chakra represents the fiery transformation of raw physical material (food) into energy. This chakra is also tied to our sense of identity. A blocked 3rd chakra can create arrogant or controlling behavior, also lethargy and depression. An open 3rd chakra allows ease with others, and high energy. The color is yellow.

4th: Heart Chakra

In your heart. This is the first higher chakra, where we feel affinity for others. Issues related to the 4th chakra move beyond the self and deal with others and divine love. A blocked 4th chakra can cut you off from your feelings and create fear of intimacy. An open 4th chakra increases your depth of life experience, brings compassion and empathy. The color is green.

5th: Throat Chakra

Located at the base of the throat, this chakra is about communication - not only verbal but also intuitive and telepathic. The 5th chakra is sometimes called a mouthpiece for the heart. It also colors the qualities of the breath, movement and sound and helps with practical intuition (messages that tell you, for example, to call a certain person). A blocked 5th chakra creates easy expression and a flood of messages, songs, phrases, poems and so on that apparently come from "nowhere". The color is blue.

6th: Brow Chakra

Located between your eyebrows, the sixth chakra represents perception and intellect, also abstract intuition for bigger details beyond the practical. This is where intellect begins to merge with higher consciousness. A blocked 6th chakra makes people become "stuck in their heads," controlling and cut off from reality. An open 6th chakra creates a sense of living in harmony with inner and outer circumstances. It is possible to have an open 6th chakra and maintain a practical life, without getting too "spaced out". The color is purple.

7th: Crown Chakra

This chakra is located at the top of the head. It represents a pure state of consciousness beyond the deta of worldly life. It is where we house our sacred beliefs. Psychic mediums also use it as the "meeting room" for spirit guides, angels and so forth. This chakra is most often activated in meditation and dreams. When blocked, the spiritual life is diminished. When open, consciousness expands.[4] The color is white.

---

[4] Chakra Subtle and Physical Connections, is reprinted with permission from <u>A Woman's Book of Balance© - Finding Your Physical, Spiritual, and Emotional Center with Yoga, Strength Training, and Dance</u> - by Karen Andes- A Perigee Book, published by The Berkley Publishing Group, Dec 1999, page 105- *www.worlddancer.com*

OPENING THE CHAKRAS THROUGH DANCE

Dancing with awareness and intent can open up your chakras and can be a powerful healing tool. Following your inner guidance and intuition, chose a special music that moves you, use your breath as your cue, and dance meditating on these definitions that embrace the

Concept of Posture

- ANCHORING - bringing your energy into your center - raise your hands on your belly,
- GROUNDING - connecting with the earth by feeling your weight on both feet,
- LOTUS FLOWER - lengthening your spine, bringing your energy up, by lifting your arms and hands above the head,
- BALLOON - expanding and opening your chest, by slowly inhaling and exhaling,
- SWAN - lengthening your neck and relax your shoulders,
- INTENT - place your intent and dance.

On the next pages I suggest how you can use the symbolism of the chakras through dancing with

Seven Veils

ENLIGHTENMENT DANCE
How Dance Can Improve the Way You Think, Feel, and Live

THE DANCE OF THE SEVEN VEILS

The enchanting story of Ishtar, Goddess of Love and Harvest (in Sumerian/Mesopotamian mythology from 4500 BC) tells us that she had to go through seven times seven gates of the underworld to save her husband Tammuz, who died and passed to the land of darkness. After every seventh gate, the price of admission was a veil, symbolizing all the things we hold dear in the mortal world. One theory of the "Dance of The Seven Veils" which Salome danced in the Old Testament is that each veil represents something which Ishtar had to sacrifice, until she was completely naked after the last gate.

Number seven is a mystical number. So many things are related to seven!

Here are a few of them:

- 7 are the colors of the rainbow
- 7 are the days of the week
- 7 are the musical notes
- 7 are the wonders of the world
- 7 are the continents of the world
- 7 are the main chakras
- 7 is the number of years a field should lay fallow during crop rotation until the soil is at its peak again
- 7 years are needed for the complete forgiveness of sin and debt, says the Old Testament
- 7 sons walking 7 times around the world, is written in Greek Mythology
- The seventh son of a seventh son is said to have extraordinary powers

No doubt there are more correspondences to the number seven in science and mysticism yet to be revealed!

The following is one of the several meanings that I have applied to the

"Dance of the Seven Veils."

AWAKENING THE CHAKRAS

I recommend silk fabric or chiffon material for a better flowing movement. Place the veils on your body according to the order 1-7 suggested below. The movements are to be performed when unveiling (or taking the veil off, before releasing it to the floor). After have them all on, perform the unveiling process as you move on a soft turn to either side. You may want to release the veils in the opposite order that you dressed them on; or just follow your intuition to which ones you will release or drop first.

Veil 1 – 2 yards red veil, placed around the hips. Symbolism: this veil represents the Root Chakra at the base of the spine, associated with passion and material needs. Suggested dance movements: hips figure eights (water and earth, see page 117• and 113•).

Affirmation: *As I release this veil, I feel secure and wealthy in all aspects of my life.*

Veil 2 – green 2 yards veil around the body tucked on the left bra strap. Suggested movement: chest movements (see page 73•) Symbolism: This veil represents the Heart Chakra.

Affirmation: *As I release the veil, I see myself moving beyond the self and any fear of intimacy. I feel compassion towards others as I overcome indecision, divisions, and fragmentations in life. By giving and receiving the energy of love I achieve balance and harmony.*

ENLIGHTENMENT DANCE
How Dance Can Improve the Way You Think, Feel, and Live

Veil 3 – lilac, 2 yards indigo blue veil, placed over the head – use a tiara or a small rubber band to hold it in place. Suggested movement: (sun disk, see page 78•). Symbolism: The 3rd eye or Brow Chakra. Dropping this veil, release and trust the Universal power. Instead of holding and controlling, let go and surrender.

Affirmation: *I open up for higher energies to emerge through me as I become aware of enlightenment.*

Veil 4 – light blue, 2 yards veil placed on the neck. Suggested movements: (cat and camel walk, see pages 75• and 77•) Symbolism: The Throat Chakra. The release of this veil amplifies perception and intuition.

Affirmation: *I am able to convey my ideas, communicating without limits.*

Veil 5 – ½ yard orange veil, hung on the right arm – use a bracelet. Suggested movements: (fire & air - the dance of the elements with hands see pages 114-116•). Symbolism: this veil represents the Pleasure Chakra.

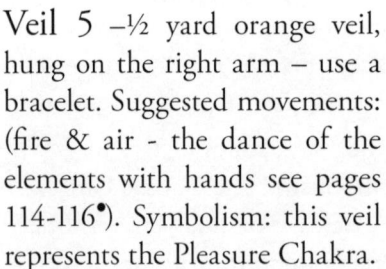

Affirmation: *As I release it, I acknowledge my sexuality, and my creativity blooms from inside out.*

Veil 6 – yellow ½ yard veil hung on the left arm – use a bracelet. Suggested movements: belly (see page 70•) Symbolism: This veil represents the Solar Plexus Chakra, at the navel, your personal power center.

Affirmation: *By dropping this veil I generate confidence, hope and bliss. I release my tendency to impose and dominate. As I let it go, I reveal my connection to others.*

Veil 7 – white or purple, 2 yards veil, over the head. Symbolism: The Crown Chakra – by releasing this last veil I achieve a holy transformation. Suggested movements: head and eyes (see page 73•)

Affirmation: *My imagination is transformed into pure spirit, creativity blossoms through every movement and moment in life. I am one with universal unconditional love.*

(Please refer to the Chakras chapter on page 49• to better understand these symbolic meanings)

(.. at the Hyatt crew lounge in Paris, March 2004)

FENG SHUI APPLIED TO DANCE

Dance Feng Shui
Dance Yin and Yang
Dance Mandala!

Feng Shui is the 5000-year-old Chinese system of arranging our environment so we can live in harmony with our surroundings. Literally, it means *wind and water*. Feng Shui can be seen as an all-embracing view of the universe, including heaven, earth, people, buildings, rooms, and energy. It can also be used to predict and support life situations such as your career, health, wealth, relationships and family life.

Feng Shui comes from Taoism, the original religion of China. The Tao is "the Way." The Chinese say that everything is the Tao, meaning everything belongs to the natural order of things. In Taoism, all things in the universe flow like a dance! From the Tao - the Way - comes all of creation. Everything we know can be divided into Heaven and Earth, or Spirit and Creation. Heaven is represented as a circle, and creation, set in the middle of heaven, as a square. This is the symbol used by the Chinese on lucky coins, and it is the inner symbol I have adopted for my dance.

From heaven (spirit), the Taoists reduced the circle to an unbroken line called yang, while creation (matter), became a broken line called yin. These two dynamic, universal co-dependant forces are depicted in the ancient Chinese symbol of Yin-Yang in perfect circular balance. Although opposites, within each there is always an element of the other... the small dot of white within the black yin, and the dot of dark within the white of the yang.

Yang & Yin, sun & shadow, summer & winter, male & female, dancing & drumming, south & north, up & down, heat & cold, hard & soft, positive & negative.. the universe of opposites generate the world of creation through balance.

Dance fast and slow, dance high and low, dance in and out, dance for you and dance for me, dance all over the stage and dance in one the spot. A real dance, like the Tao, flows with the Chi (energy). When we practice balance on the dance floor, it becomes easier to bring it to life!

Feng Shui uses an octagonal figure, called "Pah kwa." It is a chart divided into eight segments, each facing a direction and corresponding to a theme in your life:

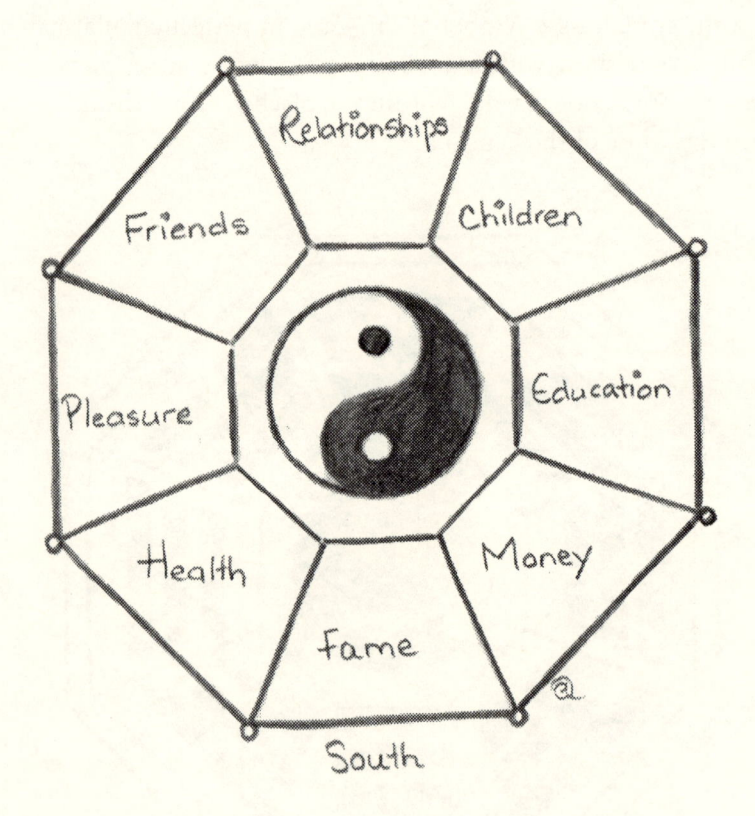

- South corresponds to prosperity and fame
- North to successful relationships
- East to wisdom and experience
- West to pleasure and indulgence
- South-East to money and wealth
- South-West to health
- North-East to children and family
- North-West to new beginnings and friends

The Pah Kwa is overlaid on a house plan and used to suggest improvements according to what falls in each area. By fixing the flow of the energy in that space, you can fix the problem related to your life in that area.

There are many books that explain how Feng Shui works. My intent here is to bring you the awareness of the principles, its yin and yang aspects. By doing this you learn to bring balance and harmony to your dance. From the dance floor to your daily life, you learn to flow with the Chi.

In the Feng Shui dance, the floor is the Pah Kwa. Draw an imaginary octagonal shaped figure and dance on it. For each area that you step, specify an intention. Breathe into it. Dance the story of each area of your life. Transform the stories that could use improvement. It is all about visualization, imagination and intention.

By dancing the Pah Kwa, you are dancing your life. You dance around the circle and on the edges, assimilating the energies that each imaginary space is honoring (follow the definitions above or create your own). Come back to center, for balance. The center is the place where your inner wisdom abides. Trust it. The center can be placed in the center of the stage or it may be located in your body. Move your hips out, and then back to center, the belly, where the inner power resides.

The Pah Kwa resembles a mandala. Mandala is the Sanskrit word for sacred circle, a symbol of creation, and "container of spirit." They are circles painted with intricate patterns and designs, used in meditation to help transcend illusion. The variety of different expressions of mandalas is infinite.

Mandalas are circular because the circle depicts the unity and endlessness of the whole of Creation. They encompass all dimensions. The light at the center of the circle is the Divine Light, which is Divine Consciousness that is omnipresent, omnipotent, and omniscient. "As above, so below." I like to see the Mandala as a blueprint of perfection.

Flowers and snowflakes are examples of naturally occurring mandalas in nature. Religious symbols such as crosses, the Star of David, and medicine wheels are mandalas. Because of their enlightening nature, mandalas inspire their use in design, ornamentation, and many other visual arts designed to unite heaven and earth. Mandalas have been used to represent divinity and promote healing and spiritual development in every culture from the beginning of time. Every aspect of a mandala has archetypal significance, and triggers ancient memories and attunement to higher qualities.

Karen Andes, in her book "A Woman's Book of Balance" teaches "The Movement Mandala." From the center, she visualizes it both as a compass and a globe. Dancing the Mandala includes honoring the directions - north, south, east and west. When you dance the directions, you can also determine the intention or meaning for each. The directions have been used by many spiritual traditions as a way of acknowledging the spirit. Here is how it is seen in Feng Shui, as an example:

> South – summer, fame and fortune
>
> North – winter, hidden, nurturing and caring
>
> West – fall, danger, strength, unpredictability
>
> East – spring, wisdom, good luck, protection

ENLIGHTENMENT DANCE
How Dance Can Improve the Way You Think, Feel, and Live

I encourage you to develop your own Mandala or Feng Shui Dance! By applying your own meanings to your dance space, you can gather inner wisdom. Once you start doing this, it becomes automatic. You will find yourself discovering meaningful and interpretive movements in your walk and gestures. You will become much more aware of your life and its events. It is like unveiling one of the greatest mysteries of life: you!

Now that you have learned the emotional and spiritual basis of dance, I encourage you to explore the different approaches. Use your dance as a moving prayer. Dance your happiness and your celebrations! Dance your sadness and your blues! Tell stories with your gestures! Dance to heal, dance to feel, and dance to express yourself!

(.. somewhere over the Pacific Ocean, October 2002)

Movement & Presentation

ENLIGHTENMENT DANCE TECHNIQUE
* Applying Intent and Developing Awareness
* Giving Meanings to Movement

BODY EXPRESSIONS

The human body can speak a non-verbal language of communication. Just by observing how people move, we can learn a lot about them. Signals like shaking the head or crossing the arms are obviously signs of disagreement. A simple smile can mean acceptance and sympathy.

A dancer communicates with the audience when she/he dances. Assigning meanings to your gestures deepen this process. The feedback is enlightening!

The Enlightenment Dancer's body represents the temple of the soul, which expresses itself in devotion from the core of one's being. The limbs may move freely and independently, or together, according to the rhythm, song and music.

Before practicing, warm up your body by stretching through a song. (Follow the Dance Meditation exercise on page 19•). Also, place yourself according to the Concept of Posture described on page 52•.

The descriptions to follow are poetic presentations of movements that we can perform with our various body parts. Please follow these suggestions for your technique guidance, but feel free to advance through the metaphors because there is always room to grow. Let your imagination fly away to capture the magic of the symbolism to your dance. You will have fun!

FEET – Feet can step so softly, with light and tender movements, or pound the earth to awaken its fertility! With our toes, we can trace sacred symbols on the floor: moons, suns, and stars. The feet are our connection to the earth, keeping us grounded. They support the whole body. They are essential to balance. They also direct energy much like the hands do. They create rhythm, sound, and vibration.

LEGS – Legs give us freedom and mobility. They are capable of moving us quickly and delicately, and of revealing our intentions through forward action. They represent impulse and will power. They also guide a dancer's direction, and as such, represent life's possibilities, paths and choices.

HIPS and BUTT – They tremble and shimmy; they move in figures-eights, circles and spirals. They make sinuous and winding movements that awaken the unknown and unconscious emotions hidden within. These curving, revolving hip movements allow the dancer to ascend with vital energy to ecstasy, promoting an inner sense of bliss. It is about accessing Heaven and Earth's energies by using moves that massage the womb they cradle.

Shimmies

<u>Hip Shimmy</u> – *This is a tremble with the hips that comes from alternating the movements of the feet and knees. The metaphor of this movement is fear. As you perform your hip shimmy, you get in touch with your fears, and beat them away with your hips.*

<u>Shoulder Shimmy</u> – *Move the shoulders forward and back quickly, alternating shoulders, one at a time. This one is a celebration movement! Share your joy with others. This shimmy is wonderfully communicative and expressive!*

<u>Whole Body Shimmy</u> – *Press your feet to the floor and tighten up your thighs and buttock muscles. Move your knees in and out creating a vibration that travels up to your whole body.*

The shimmy says, "Release the fear and let go of control"

STOMACH / BELLY / WOMB

The belly is the power center of the body, as we stand on earth at the pivot point between the heavens and the underworld. It is also where we were connected - literally, person to person - to our mother by the umbilical cord. If the belly is relaxed, but strong and active, our whole system works better: we will breathe and digest easier; have more beautiful skin, and avoid back pain!

The belly muscles, including the diaphragm, control our breath. The womb is the source of creation. It pulses, vibrates, shakes and undulates! A fountain of energy, the womb embodies the magic of generating life. By undulating the belly muscles upwards, we raise energy skyward; undulating it downwards, we send energy into the earth, thus creating balance during the dance, like the sun and moon, day and night, light and dark, heaven and earth, celebration and quietude – this is the feng shui principles applied into the dance (see page 60*).

Learning to move through the belly and to breathe through it, allows us to gain control and a sense of vigor and radiance. Both undulations and flutters require diaphragmatic breathing.

Here is a simple exercise will develop control of the abdominal muscles, and naturally lead to beautiful undulations in your dance:

Inhaling through the nose, drop the diaphragm and expand the belly; don't fill the chest, let the dropping diaphragm make room for your lungs to expand downward. Exhale, squeezing the air out of your belly with your stomach muscles.

Belly "flutters" come from breathing out, empting the air from the belly, and doing a sucking action from the throat. When you apply intent to your movements, you learn to control the energies of your body. For example, undulating the belly upwards can promote an ecstatic happy energy, bringing a state of joy and celebration. On the other hand, undulating down, calms people down, bringing the energy to a quieter state. You can actually change the atmosphere in a room with your intentional dance movements. So, if a group is too excited, use soothing, soft, subtle movements, like undulating your belly downwards, to relax them. If they are too serious, rational and judgmental, use exciting actions and move your belly upwards, to lift the energy up to a more vibrant and participatory level. These moves affect the energy because of the intent you apply to them. I have verified this through my own experience with many audiences.

BREASTS

Women's breasts express universal maternal love, sensuality, and divine, life-giving sacrifice. Men's chests convey strength, paternal love, protection, and expansive passion. The Chest can also undulate, expand and contract. Every breath gives us an opportunity to lift our chest. The chest houses the heart, pumping blood to our whole body. By lifting our chest we balance our body's energy and reassure self-esteem. How can we love others if we have our heart closed down with poor posture? By lifting your chest the breathing is no longer shallow. It becomes full and sublime.

SHOULDERS

The shoulders represent the intention to help humanity grow into a more connected world of enlightenment and bliss. By moving the shoulders we immediately connect with the audience. It is a movement of getting out from the self to engage the other: *Hello, I am here!*

Move your shoulders with the music, fast or slow, sensuously or subtly. The shoulders embody communication, our interaction with people.

ARMS

Arms can give the impression that the dancer is as light as a bird, flying into the sky, leaving the earth behind; or she is a graceful swimmer, gliding through the sea; or a strong warrior, ready to fight; or a lover, ready to embrace. Move your arms from the shoulders out, and imagine strings attached to your hips. Use a smooth and fluid movement.

HANDS

The dancer's hands simulate flowers, water, fire, birds, scorpions, cats, and serpents.. expressing a non-verbal language of movements speaking of all nature's aspects.

Notice the three parts of your hands: wrist, center and fingers. Move one part at a time. Again, make a conscious effort to create smooth movements.

FINGERS

Moved from the wrist, the fingers glide through the air, like flower petals, drawing the most delicate shapes: figure-eights, spirals, waves and even letters of the alphabet that form invisible, speechless words, in endless forms of motion. Use the sections of the fingers independently.

HEAD

The head can seem to "dislocate" from the body, each vertebra articulated independently, giving a serpentine effect. The head can move from side to side, or front to back. It can tilt and turn, showing how we orient ourselves. Wherever we are is the "center" of our Universe, and we find that center by looking at what surrounds us. What we are looking at is where our attention is in life at that moment, and we look "a-head" to where we are going.

Moving the head sideways (the "Egyptian Slide") represents attention to what is going on in the present moment, and gives new perspectives on it – seeing things from different sides. Sliding the head side to side brings our awareness into the present moment. Being present - acknowledging what's happening in the now - gives more meaning to life; knowledge to be acquired (as if you were stretching to look deeper into the future). When we move the head front to back, it shows reflection on the past and the future.

EYES

Your eyes are the mirrors of your soul. They also clearly show the direction of your attention. Eyes are very expressive and magnetic. Let your eyes shine during your dance!

- Looking <u>left</u> represents <u>reverence to the moon</u>, meaning sensibility, intuition, creativity, and remembrance of the history of humanity.

- Glancing <u>right</u> symbolizes <u>reverence to the sun</u>, meaning hope for the future, attention and awareness of finding new ways to achieve fulfillment in life.

CHEST

The chest houses our heart. When moving the chest, we can express our deepest emotions: love, sorrow, joy, and pain. We connect with our compassion and feelings of gratitude towards the universe. I like to say that the chest is our "sun." It should be up and shining, by opening our arms wide and expanding our chest. It is like opening your heart to the infinite dimensions of love.

Types of movements with the chest: circles, figure eights, letters of the alphabet, lifts and drops, using the rib cage and the breath.

ENLIGHTENMENT DANCE
How Dance Can Improve the Way You Think, Feel, and Live

WALKS AND STEPS

Cat Walk

Slide toes on the floor as you move forward, hands moving up and down (as described at page 111*) imitating a cat.

This movement symbolizes the mystery of the unknown.

Scorpion Walk

One foot moves forward and back, while the other steps forward. This movement represents the yin and the yang aspects of life, the duality of sun and moon, day and night, man and woman, give and receive, out and in, forward and back. It means balance in all aspects of life.

Camel Walk

Move with one foot behind the other with an upper torso undulation, moving the pelvis in and out, alternating with the chest. Like the camel crossing the desert: plodding on under any circumstances, not stopping for rain, storm, catastrophes, the camel step-step-steps across the desert.

The meaning of this movement is "life goes on..."

Scarab Beetle

A hip thrust, walking forward (like a washing machine). For the ancient Egyptians, the Sacred Scarab Beetle was the first signal of the budding springtime (like the robin is to us)!

The meaning of this move is hope, new beginnings, and celebration!

Sun Disk

This movement is a turn around with a kick. It means change in life, because the sun rises and sets, and there are always new dawns. So, move on and acknowledge new possibilities by kicking away the old ones. Place your weight on the left foot, bend both knees, lean back your torso and kick sideways with the right foot, as you rotate around yourself. (Alternate sides)

Half Moon

Here we back-step by drawing an imaginary half moon on the floor with the toe. Place your weight on the left foot and point your right toe forward, dragging it back on the floor in a half-moon shape. Shift the body weight to the other foot and repeat.

The meaning is introspection, going inwards to find balance, getting time and space for yourself.

ENLIGHTENMENT DANCE
How Dance Can Improve the Way You Think, Feel, and Live

You can apply different meanings to your body limbs or you can follow those I've suggested. It is important to understand that the deeper you get involved in doing this, the more you will tune in to your intuition and the present moment. It is as if you have found a whole new approach to life.. as if life is unfolding itself in the dance. As you learn to give meaning to your movements, your life gains meaning by itself. I also believe that applying natural meanings to the movements brings an ecstatic power to energize and heal us.

(..Orlando Airport, February, 2002)

Telling Stories through Dance

TELLING STORIES THROUGH DANCE

THE DANCER

Once came to the court of the Prince of Birkasha a dancer with her musicians. And she was admitted to the court, and she danced before the prince to the music of the lute and the flute and the zither.

She danced the dance of flames, and the dance of swords and spears; she danced the dance of stars and the dance of space. And then she danced the dance of flowers in the wind.

After this she stood before the throne of the Prince and bowed her body before him. And the Prince bade her to come nearer, and he said unto her:

"Beautiful woman, daughter of grace and delight, whence comes your art? And how is it that you command all the elements in your rhythms and your rhymes?"

And the dancer bowed again before the Prince, and she answered:

"Mighty and gracious Majesty, I know not the answer to your questionings. Only this I know: The philosopher's soul dwells in his head, the poet's soul is in the heart, the singer's soul lingers about his throat, but the soul of the dancer abides in all her body"

Khalil Gibran

STORIES FROM THE PAST

THE STORY OF ISIS AND OSIRIS

I have often found inspiration in the mythical tales from ancient Egypt. The stories of the gods Isis and Osiris particularly have always fascinated me! It was with my first belly dance teacher in Brazil, Regina Ferrari, that I learned movements that express this story. I have danced it in many ways, with different kinds of music, in a variety of settings. I love using the myths of Isis and Osiris to teach my students how to tell stories through dance. Here, I share these movements with you, in the hopes they may help you create your own mythical dance!

In Ancient Egypt, it was told how Isis, "Goddess of the Moon" and Osiris the "Sun God" were in love, and happily married.

ENLIGHTENMENT DANCE
How Dance Can Improve the Way You Think, Feel, and Live

The Movement:

Start the dance wrapped in a veil.

Bring the veil from the back around your body and stick the left edge under your bra or vest. Bring the right edge across the left and tuck in under the left bra or vest.

Perform an unveiling. Hold the left edge and pull it off as you turn to the right, opening it up.

Turn to the right again, and you are now facing forward with the veil totally opened on your back.

Metaphoric meaning: the mysteries of "Isis" and "Osiris" are like the mysteries of life, they can be reveled to you if you open up and tune in to your intuition.

1) Isis is very happy. Her symbol is a white bird flying in the sky. She shows her delight by smiling, leaning, reaching and side-stepping in alternating directions, with pointed toes and fluttering veil.

The movement:

Starting with your weight on your left foot, stretch your right leg towards the right, toes pointing down. With veil in both hands, extend your arms and lift the veil towards the right, wafting it into the air, arms outstretched, with the body undulating in a side step.

As you bring the veil down, billowing full of air, gracefully step onto the pointed toes of the right foot. Do this twice in rocking rhythm with the music. Then turn left and repeat the same veil-waving step twice in that direction. Alternate direction again, waving and stepping twice. You can slowly turn and walk-step Isis' "flight" through the air.

Metaphoric Meaning: Like Isis, feel free like a bird. Smile, enjoying the moments of life.

2) Osiris appears. He is the guardian of the Earth. In one hand he holds a staff and in the other a whip; they are crossed at face level, in a protective stance, with the veil making a fence or shield around his body.

The Movement: *Walk confidently forward, deliberately crossing one foot in front of the other, placing the souls flat on the ground. Perform several stately steps forward as Osiris.*

Metaphoric meaning: Be strong and protect yourself in case you face a life-battle. Feel your male, grounding strength. You have the power to fight for what you want.

3) Osiris and Isis were together with Ra, the God of Creation.

The movement: *With the veil in both hands, throw it high up towards the right and look up, while lifting up the left leg behind you, knee bent, foot kicking up, toes pointing towards the sky. Pull the veil down, bend, and bring the back foot down at the same time. Repeat this lift-and-bend towards the right and towards the left.*

Metaphoric meaning: You are never alone; feel the presence of divine powers, your angels, your spiritual guides, protecting and leading you.

4) Seth, the God of the desert and the underworld appears.
He stands with hands joined overhead, the veil falling behind. Seth is jealous of Isis and Osiris' love affair, and he kills Osiris, thus bringing darkness to the world.

The movement:

Cross the feet, bend your knees, and make a dramatic, sweeping forward bend, bowing with your arms, head and hair falling down, veil trailing all the way down to the floor. Open the veil wide across the floor, close it again, and sweep it back up overhead, then open it behind you, standing with arms outstretched.

Metaphoric meaning: Remember that life has its ups and downs. Be willing to accept this, and be aware that after going down, you will always come up again. Like resurrecting, like rebirthing. The winter will always eventually end, allowing the spring may return.

5) Isis cries and her tears make the Nile River overflow its banks.

The movement:

Stand with the back of the right hand at the forehead, indicating grief. The right leg is bent and poised before the left, with toes pointing and touching the ground.

Isis' sobbing is shown as trembling of the belly: Breathe rapidly, with quick, shallow breaths, shimmying in and out (inhaling expands the belly, exhaling tightens it).

With a "half-moon" rotation of the forward knee, shift to the other leg and direction, and repeat.

Metaphoric Meaning: Feel the emotions. If you feel sad, cry. Digest your feelings. Let your emotions flow. (Otherwise they stagnate in your body and can become chronic illness, such as ulcers, head aches, even cancer.)

6) The God of the Afterlife, Jacal, also known as Anubis, arrives to help. Isis is inspired to summon her regenerative powers and bring Osiris back to life.

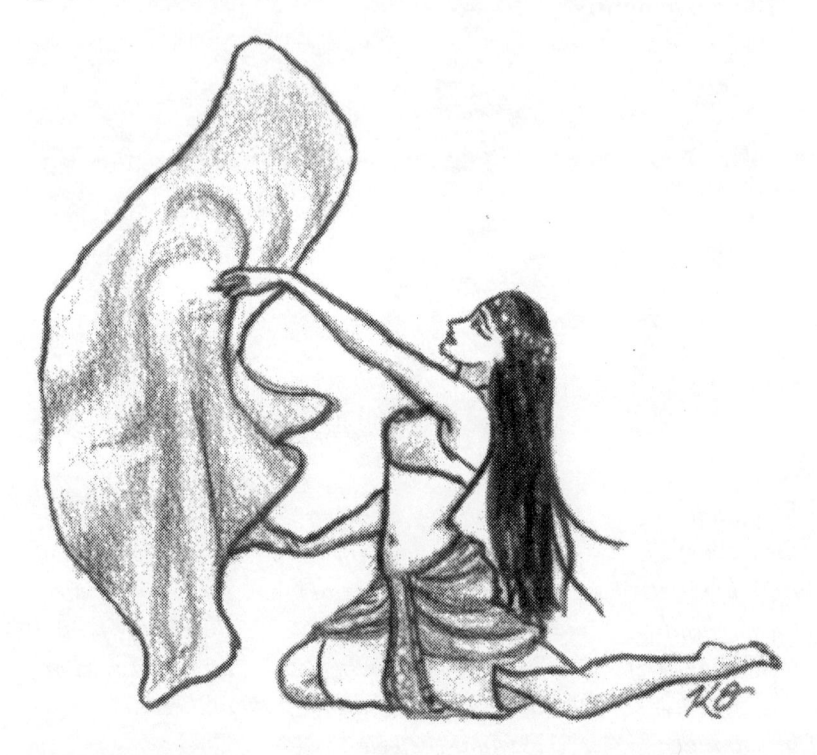

The movement: *Kneel down, one knee deeply bent, the other leg outstretched behind. Wave the veil with arms moving in opposite directions, up and down, creating a turbulence, symbolizing transformation. Repeat, kneeling on the other knee, in opposite direction.* Osiris is resurrected from the bottom of the river by Isis' love.

Metaphoric meaning: If you face a life-challenging situation, you will be able to find strength if you focus on doing so. You can do anything; trust your inner guidance.

7) Isis and Osiris conceive a baby.

The movement:

Standing with right leg forward, arms out to your side, make undulating <u>upward</u> belly-rolling movements. Keep the breath flowing.

The baby is born: Sweep the right leg back and reverse the belly-rolling movements to go <u>downwards</u>.

Metaphoric meaning: Get in touch with your breath. Bring your thoughts to your belly. Digest your problems to create solutions. Live life fully. Feel everything. Be open to your creativity. Make things happen. Conceive and give birth to your ideas!

8) The child is Horus, the Falcon God. He challenges and destroys Seth, taking control of the earth for the good and peace of all.

The movement:

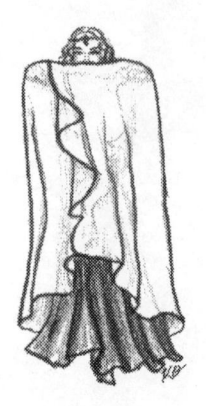

Begin with the same protective arm position that Osiris had: Hands up at the face, drawing the veil into a wrap-around shield.

Lift one leg way up, knee bending towards the chest, toes pointing down. Then perform a high-stepping forward walk. As each leg lifts, throw the veil open wide. As each foot steps down and crosses forward, close the veil in front of the face again.

Lift the veil in both hands together overhead. Stand and gyrate hands, arms, and torso, like a tornado. By slightly bending the legs, raise and lower the rotating "storm," which cleanses the world of evil.

Metaphoric meaning: Trust that you can change anything. Life is a choice. Every minute you have the chance to fight for your dreams.

9) The God of Air, "Shu" circulates in all directions for blessings.

The movement: *Sweep the veil around your head in large circles while twirling around like a hurricane. Make overhead figure eights with the hands palm out, circulating in rhythm with your hip circles.*

Metaphoric meaning: Go for it! Don't waste your time. Move on!

10) Life goes on, just like a camel walking persistently across the desert.

The Movement: *One foot takes small steps, staying ahead, and draws the other towards it in a forward slide across the floor. The torso and belly undulate with each step. You can reverse directions, and also "camel walk" around in a small circle.*

Metaphoric Meaning: Remember, life goes on, whatever happens. The sun will come up in the morning; the moon will come out at night. "Camel-walk" through life's path.

ENLIGHTENMENT DANCE
How Dance Can Improve the Way You Think, Feel, and Live

11) The Goddess of Justice, "Maat" observes and judges all.

The movement:

Start with the hands symbolizing her headdress of feathers, high overhead, close together but with fingers splayed outwards.

Bring the arms down, outstretched to your side, like the beams of a scale, rocking, symbolizing Maat's fair observation and impartial judgment.

"Camel walk" sideways, with this arm gesture of balance, first right, then left.

Metaphoric meaning: Balance. The best way is the middle way. Don't take extreme actions. Not too much, not too little.

12) "Geb," The Earth Goddess, transmits stability and security to all.

The movement:

Bring the middle of the veil across the front of the neck and drape its two ends back over your shoulders. Your arms are held freely out and a bit forward, in an open embrace. Sweep the right leg out right around and behind you, and kneel down on the right knee. As that knee folds and takes your weight, bend and sweep the left leg back as well, knee partially bent. (You are sitting on the floor in a "side-saddle" position.)

Then throw your head and hair and arms forward and down to the ground, and sweep in a wide, low arc across the floor. The hands create beautiful caressing movements. Raise the torso, throw back your head and hair, reach up overhead, waving the hands and arms; then reach forward and lower the body back down, the hands and arms cascading to the ground.

Perform this earth-sweeping circle several times, then reverse your folded legs into the opposite "side-saddle" position and repeat. Get up slowly by bringing one leg forward, kneeling, then standing.

Metaphoric meaning: Grounding. Stay present and aware of your life's needs. Remember, you are a divine spirit incarnated in a human body. Feel the energies of Mother Earth within your being. Be blessed by it. Exchange and embrace this grounding energy.

13) "Ka" is the symbol of healing energy and it's power to help humanity. World peace is restored.

The movement:

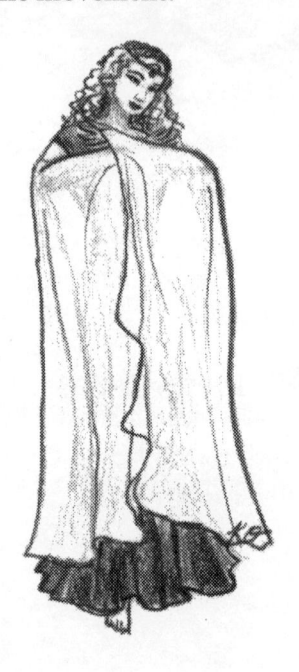

The veil is still draped across the neck and over the shoulders, or simply around your back.. Hold each corner at the heart, then with one forward step, make an opening gesture with both arms from the heart towards the people.

Gracefully bring the same foot back behind you as you close the veil over the heart. Repeat this forward and back stepping, first revealing, then covering the heart each time.

Metaphoric Movement: Give and receive. Love and be loved. Externalize, then introspect; a time for others, and a time for yourself. Balance.

ENLIGHTENMENT DANCE
How Dance Can Improve the Way You Think, Feel, and Live

14) "Ra" sends the boat that travels the world, rescuing the "good ones" and destroying the "bads."

The movement: *Step lightly around in a large circle, dragging your veil across the floor, ending in a small spin.*

Metaphoric meaning: If you are awake, you awake others by example. Bring others to find and share the light with you!

15) **The dancers show gratitude and devotion to the Goddess Isis for restoring love and bringing the Guardian, Horus to the world.**

The Movement:

Place the left leg well forward, knee slightly bent, toes pointing down and touching the floor. The right leg is behind you, knee bent. Beginning with hands crossed over the chest,

look and reach up overhead to the sky.

Lean well backwards and drop the veil, symbolizing the end of winter and the liberation of Spring. Then with a graceful, "pulling" motion, draw the moon energy of Isis down into your heart, expressing great appreciation.

Metaphoric Meaning: Be thankful for everything that you have: your health, your friends and family. Appreciate the food you eat. Be thankful for your body, which is able to dance.

Feel gratitude for the whole universe!

ENLIGHTENMENT DANCE
How Dance Can Improve the Way You Think, Feel, and Live

DANCING CONTEMPORARY LIFE STORIES

Seeing My Job through Dance…

"THE FLIGHT ATTENDANT DANCE"

I enjoy dancing like our ancient ancestors did, inspired by everyday life, learning new movements and giving them meaning! I also love bringing traditional dance into a 21st century perspective. By observing our modern surroundings, I can tell new-age versions of timeless stories. From this perspective, the dance I create is also ageless, a story that lives in our collective body-memories. Bringing the old to meet the new opens channels for the evolutionary process to take place in our world.

Like most people, I experienced fear after the drastic events of September 11, 2001. I used to love my job as a Flight Attendant, but I thought I would never fly again. It was only through dance that I regained the courage to return. Instead of continuing to mourn about that terrible episode, I started to tune in to the bliss that I originally felt when flying. I remembered the wonderful moments I shared with passengers and colleagues throughout my career, and imagined that

I was still flying with them. Then I realized that some of the routine movements of our work on the plane reminded me of ancient belly dance moves!

Every now and then, a scene would come to my mind and I would portray it as if it were a dance. Soon I had choreographed a whimsical routine that tells the story of a Flight Attendant working on the plane. By doing this I brought the past into the present moment and released my fear.

As a Flight attendant, I am fascinated by flying. A commercial jet airliner at 35,000 feet is a unique environment: a confined space with no frontier. Inside the airplane there are no national divisions, no racial segregation, no religious distinctions. But there is a financial division. If you have the money, you sit in a comfortable seat that converts to an even cozier bed at the touch of a button. The less privileged sit crushed between other unfortunate passengers, with little wiggle room. Only occasionally do rich people travel in Economy, or are people of modest means lucky enough to win an "upgrade" to First Class.

An airplane cabin requires its own movements and rhythms, and the entire flight truly looks like a dance! In the tiny little economy-class galley, the rhythm is *staccato*! Just one Flight Attendant in each galley is responsible for preparing the food for almost 300 people on a fully booked 777 aircraft! She or he has to move quickly in a confined space between hot ovens! Here, all kinds of rhythms occur at the same time! Depending on where you are seated and who is also crushed beside you, things can get pretty hot, and the rhythms can go from "Carnival" to "Zaar" (Egyptian rhythm for exorcism). If you brought some sleeping pills, you could fly "Zen." But if you like to drink, you can easily disturb your Zen neighbor!

On the other hand, in the First Class cabin, Flight Attendants serve caviar and champagne in a lyrical, *sophisticated* movement, like astronauts floating in space! In Executive Class, the movements are more *fluid* and constant, with not as much time to stop between offering a chocolate bar and smiling.

ENLIGHTENMENT DANCE
How Dance Can Improve the Way You Think, Feel, and Live

Especially on long international trips, Flight Attendants have to work within all these rhythms for hours on end. To function effectively inside that confined space, with no rest or escape, is a real challenge! But, if you know how to *dance,* it makes all the difference! The "dance" that happens on an airplane is also the dance of Life. We only have to "tune-in" to see it!

This dance creation, "The Flight Attendant Dance" has become a signature presentation for the Enlightenment Dance Company. It is a healing dance, created with the intent to transmute fear after the tragic events of 9/11. Each movement has meaning, and it is the ultimate modern dance, since its original dance floor was the galley of a 777, the most advanced aircraft in the world!

The Flight Attendant Dance that I have created was inspired by my years of experience on the job in the air. The airlines are still hurting from that moment when the world was shown how fragmented, isolated, and vulnerable we "civilized" humans have become. Today, inside the planes, I see the conflict, insecurity and fear in travelers' eyes. It is not just fear of flying. It is deeper than that. I believe it is a fear of not knowing the way back..

Who knows the way back to that "paradise land," that realm where peace abides? The Flight Attendant Dance brings us closer. When the only "goal" is play, we forget everything else and dance the fullness of the moment. Because only the present moment contains the solutions we are looking for!

That is why I dance.

There's nothing better then being in the moment to enjoy the beauty of life! Most flight attendants naturally learn how to do this: Our job is all about NOW: responding to changes in the weather, crew schedules, mechanics, passengers and much more!

To be in the moment is to let go. Focusing on this present moment frees us from the unknown. It's like breathing. If we don't notice the here and now, it is gone forever, never to return. It is by focusing on the moment that we can appreciate the beauty of a flower, or a nice conversation at the "jump seat" (the seat where the Flight Attendants sit on the plane for take-off and landing).

Sometimes, flight attendants too find it hard to live in the moment. Stress gets to us, blocking our ability to see beyond the confusion and live life fully. It is well known that one of the best stress-busters is exercise. Some people work out, others walk, or run, or swim. I dance!

Dance puts me fully present in the moment. The rhythms that I love catch me, take me away with my breath, and suddenly I am one with the dance: there's no tomorrow, no yesterday... just the eternal now. I've learned that dance is one of the best ways to heal negative emotions. Through dance, I release tension; I celebrate life and movement! Dance brings enlightenment! It is a feeling of eternal bliss!

On my layover in different places of the world, I look for opportunities to learn new forms of cultural dance and the meaning dances hold for the native people. I have been sharing what I learn from my travels and studies with my students and other Flight Attendants. I especially love creating choreographies that apply to our day-to-day lives.

So, I was inspired to create a dance that tells the story of the Flight Attendant's job at 35 thousand feet! This dance is fun, aerobic, easy to learn, and has all the phases of the flight: The Boarding Walk dance, the Kick-the-Terrorist-Away step, the Galley Dance, the Chicken-or-Beef move, the Turbulence-and-Compliance Check walk, the Pickup Dance, the Salute to the Airports, Tribute to the Union and Homage to the Company dances, and finally, the Landing Pose! What fun, making dance out of our every-day jobs!

Darkness does not exist where there is light. When we tune in to this spiritual reality, we are freed from our fears, and protected by the magic power of love. I invite you to get on board Enlightenment Airlines, "The Airline that frees the spirit!" and dance with me![5]

---

[5] *The Flight Attendant Dance is now available on video. If you would like to learn this choreography, contact: www.RosaneGibson.com

ENLIGHTENMENT DANCE
How Dance Can Improve the Way You Think, Feel, and Live

I encourage you to create your own dance based on your life story or based on another story you enjoyed reading, or maybe on someone else's life story! Transform your life into a dance by interpreting its episodes into dance movements! Start by looking at everything and everyone through enlightening rhythms!

DANCING THE FOUR ELEMENTS

Earth, Fire, Air, Water

Honoring the traditional four major natural "elements"[6] through dance is a way of getting in touch with nature and spirit. It turns our awareness to the life force within, and teaches us how to connect to it. Dancing with the intention of touching various aspects of nature brings energy and vigor to our life. It heightens intuition and our self-healing powers.

---

[6] The ancient notion of "elements" differs from that depicted in the modern scientific Periodic Table of the Elements. The five natural elements - earth, water, fire, air, and ether - correspond to what are now referred to as the "phases" of matter - solid, liquid; gas, and plasma (superheated matter, at the heart of stars, for example); and ether is invisible energy that pervades the Universe.

ENLIGHTENMENT DANCE
How Dance Can Improve the Way You Think, Feel, and Live

The movements below are symbolic representations of the elements that I have found to work for me. Please use them as inspirational guidelines if you wish. The reason I associate each movement to an element is because this brings me the sense of that element. Please feel free to innovate and create your own symbolic movement. You too can develop your own metaphoric movements, by opening up to your creativity.

Once you have learned how to focus energy through your body, you may find various props to be exciting extensions of your movements and creative expression. I also like to relate my props to the dance of the elements. Following are the elements, and the corresponding movements with body parts and props, associated with metaphoric symbolism for enlightenment.

I also feel that the elements can correspond to the phases of life we experience over time. For this reason, I have invited my students Alana, Nichole and Janet to model and demonstrate these movements for you. Alana represents the earth in her childhood. Nichole represents fire in her youthfulness. I represent air in my adulthood and Janet is water in her maturity. All of us dancing together represent the fifth element ether.

Here are the basic structures for the movements proposed:

How the Hips Move

Let's use the <u>figure-eight</u> to move the hips. The eight (8) is an ancient symbol of infinity, of never ending circles. It was adopted by the ancient Egyptians because it represented eternity and life after death. Nature has always been filled with spirals, circles, semi-circles, and figures-eights. They are everywhere, in spider webs, plants, seashells, and in the movements of animals such as snakes, birds, insects, etc. We can see these shapes on the sky: the planets, the sun, the moon! Even the cells of our body have circular shapes. Connecting to the symbol of eight and circles bring subconscious resonance to nature and the universe to which we belong.

☞ Move your hips as if they were paint brushes painting eights on the floor, or on the wall in front of you.

How the Hands Dance

<u>Hand Waves</u>: Think of the hand as segmented in three parts: heel, center, and fingers. Move one segment up at a time, in order (heel, center, fingers), producing an undulating wave-like motion.

<u>Wrist Circles</u>: Fingers are together, but not tense, with thumb also close in to the others. Gracefully rotate the wrist in wide circles, as if you are cleaning out the inside of a round pot.

☞ While dancing, combine both hand waves and wrist circles. Feel the energy flowing through your hands.

DANCING THE FOUR ELEMENTS WITH HANDS AND HIPS

EARTH

Earth is the element of strength. It supports our bodies, feeds us, and shelters us. It is solid, stable and dependable. It is the realm of abundance and prosperity. The Earth represents the physical, material plane, and it supports all the other elements. Earth is related to the sense of touch. Drums translate the Earth's heartbeat. To me, the word "earth" resonates with the body, healing and nature's power, the sense of touch, money, growth, prosperity and stability, birth, death, rocks, crystals and jewels, bones and metals. The healing power of the element earth is to ground and to bring material security. When dancing the earth element, tune in to the idea of being alive and having all your material needs fulfilled.

HAND MOVEMENT SYMBOLIZING EARTH

The hands start down by your side, towards the earth, and move as if you are scooping out holes with circular wrist movements (following the hand dance explained above).

Keeping the wrist and hand movements going, begin to slowly and gracefully raise the right hand up in front of you, like the stem of a plant growing from the earth, past the belly and heart, to the face. Your face is the flower. Move your head gently from side to side, while the hand creates a moving "frame" surrounding it. Then bring the right hand down again, and repeat the upward sequence with the left.

HIP MOVEMENT SYMBOLIZING EARTH

The imaginary figure-eight is horizontally placed below your feet. The hip movements for dancing the Earth element are wide lateral rotations to front (forward), side and center (in that order). Repeat this sequence, smoothly alternating the left and right side-rolling movements with each cycle: *front, right side, center,* and then *front left side center.* Keep the knees comfortably bent and feel grounded to the Earth. The feet are together and "rooted," and do not move.

FIRE

Fire is the heat of desire, sensuality and passion. It represents both a sexual fire and a divine enlightenment that is shining within. The source of light, it is the most spiritual of the elements. It is a chemical reaction, and as such its magic is the processes of change and transformation. It can be threatening and scary, but its results can also be spectacular, like the mythical Phoenix bird rising from its own ashes. Fire is the warrior that abides inside us.

Fire reminds me of the desert, volcanoes, saunas, candles, fireworks and fireplaces. It corresponds to the youthful phase of our lives. Summer represents fire. Musically, I associate fire with the stringed instruments.

Dancing with fire fills me with the brilliant energy of spirit, the heat of the soul and blood. It brings the power to transmute and heal, the chance to destroy and rebuild, inner vision, illumination, explosions, love and passion, transformation, protection, courage and power. Dance with fire and learn that you are indestructible! Whatever happens in your life only makes you stronger!

HAND MOVEMENT SYMBOLIZING FIRE

Place yourself in a profile position. Bring the elbows together in front of you, bent, with forearms up. With the hands facing each other, create a flaming movement by undulating them together (wrist.. center.. finger). Start this flame high in the air and draw it down before you (keeping the forearms vertical and elbows near each other). Repeatedly trace the flame, always from above down. Complete the "fire stance" by putting your weight on your left leg and extending the right foot away from the body, toes pointing to the floor, creating a long, graceful arch with the whole body, from outstretched toes to your head and arms.

HIP MOVEMENT SYMBOLIZING FIRE

The hip movement for fire duplicates an imaginary figure-eight vertically: Lift the right hip up, then move it out away from the body, then down and back in. Repeat from the left hip. Tracing this figure-eight motion from the hips, dip the body down by bending the knees, then reverse the figure-eight, and stand back up.

AIR

Air represents the intellect. It is thought-forms, the breath of creation, and the words of communication. Air also signifies freedom, intuition, inspiration, travel, the fairies that inhabit the world of wind, mountaintops, and flowers. Air is the atmosphere around us, and is intimately connected to our senses of smell and hearing. Incense and wind instruments such as the flute invoke the images of clouds, wind, and sky. These can all be represented visually in the beautiful, billowing, fluttering veil, as can the spirit of air-dwelling birds, such as the noble eagle and the swift, keen-eyed falcon! When I dance the element air I feel mature and powerful. It's an "all knowing feeling" of gratitude, serenity, intuitive awareness.

HAND MOVEMENT SYMBOLIZING AIR

The hands gently caress the air before you, about two feet apart, palms facing each other. They undulate parallel with each other, from side to side, as if being swept like the branches of a tree in the wind. This wide, side-to-side rocking motion can dip below the waistline, or across your front, or over your head. Let the knees flex and the whole body sway. You can also allow the "wind" to turn you completely around in a spin.

HIP MOVEMENT SYMBOLIZING AIR

The imaginary figure-eight is at the side of the hip. The hip and leg motion for dancing the air element involves tracing a large, open figure-eight with pointed toes away from the body, just above the floor. Do this first from one leg, then the other.

WATER

Water is the element of purification, of love and all emotions. Our emotions flow like water, in eternal movement and change. Water also symbolizes the subconscious, also ever moving, like the ocean, day and night creating waves that we only barely perceive consciously - the waves of life, the power of purification and inner wisdom. Water in all its myriad forms -ocean, lake, river, ice, snow, fog, rain, - reveals to me feelings of love, persistence, tenderness, sadness, intuition, spirituality, dreaminess, friendship, and inner reflection. Water is purifying; it is flowing; it is healing; it is soft and lovely, always in motion!

Water represents the life-phase of adulthood. The elementals are undines, other water fairies and mermaids. It is related to the sense of taste. It is often symbolized by the lotus flower and dolphins. Its musical instruments are the piano and flute.

Water flows in rivers and on the crashing waves of the ocean. It falls from the sky in drops of rain. Water is totally mutable as it changes state. It can be frozen solid or hot vapor. Water brings the power of intuition and the flexibility to adjust to daily life. When we cry, water flows from our eyes. When we sweat it releases stress and heat from the body. Our bodies are 80% water. We can't live without it. If you tune in to the powerful essence of the symbolism of water, you will learn that sometimes you need to be strong and solid, like ice, other times you have to be soft and transparent like vapor. Just let yourself flow like the waves of the ocean. Dance with water jars in your hands or create movements that can put you in tune with the element water.

HAND MOVEMENT SYMBOLIZING WATER

The hands are palms down, fingers extended and together. Their movement is like waves coming from the arms out through the three hand sections (heels, palms, then fingers). Move the hands up and down together. Varying the height of the lift, you can duplicate little waves, bigger ones, or huge, overhead waves. Once you have mastered the water movement of the hands, allow the whole body to follow.. as if dipping, lifting, and leaning far forward and back, like a surging tide.

HIP MOVEMENT SYMBOLIZING WATER

The hip movement for the water element is similar to the Earth's but it is more exaggerated ("wavy"), and it starts with a *backward* scoop instead of forward. Also, the heel of the foot on each side you sway towards lifts up, leaving only the toes touching the floor. Feel your body weight (80% water) sloshing side to side, moving you like a floating boat.

DANCING THE FOUR ELEMENTS WITH PROPS

Tambourines, Drums & Flower Basket Symbolizing Earth

Tambourines and drums appeal to me as "earthy" instruments. When I dance with them, I place the intent of this connection and feel the earth energy that these percussion instruments transmit.

Dancing with flowers is similar. I use either artificial or real flowers. I like to dance with flower baskets or dress up with lots of flowers to connect with the earth element. I use movements that honor these props. I dance around them, frame them with my hands as if the props (not me), were the most important part of the dance. I play the tambourines and the drums when I dance with them, synchronizing the beat of the song with my heart.

Candles, Candelabra, Fire Buttons Or Flashlight Symbolizing Fire

Candelabras are also called Shemadan. The Egyptians began dancing with them in the early 20th century. It is part of the Egyptian wedding ritual, but many couples of other Middle Eastern nationalities have adopted it as part of their wedding celebration, incorporating it along with their own rituals. This procession traditionally occurs at night, winding its way through the streets of the neighborhood from the home of the bride's parents to her new home at the groom's house. This is the official moving of the bride and is led by a dancer, musicians and singers, followed by the wedding party and their friends and family. The dancer does her full theatrical candelabra dance, including floor work, and gets everyone dancing together. The meaning is showing the light, lighting up the way for the bride and groom. I use this meaning every time I perform with the Candelabra. I believe this is the symbolism of fire dance: to light up the way... enlightenment!

☞ When dancing with fire props, be careful! Make sure that it is safe to do so.

Be creative! I like to place a little tea light candle inside a wine glass (one for each hand) and dance with them on my hands. Other times I enjoy the power of placing a huge nine candle holder candelabrum on my head, or dancing with finger extensions with cotton wraps on fire!

Flashlights are also a wonderful substitute for real fire and they can produce a similar effect. I have performed with neon lights and it was fantastic! The dance becomes very powerful and hypnotic for both dancer and audience!

Finger Cymbals Representing Air

Musical tones can have healing properties, and even seem to purify the environment, in the sense of "clearing the air." When we have discussions and arguments, negative thought-forms can permeate the atmosphere of a house. Vibrating bells (high or low pitched) can dissipate such psychic pollution. I believe this is why bells are so prevalent in churches and temples. They not only signal the time of service and put people in the proper frame of mind; they create a sacred space. Bell tones are refreshing and energetic. Listening to a clear, beautiful bell ringing feels like getting cleansed inside and out.

When we dance with finger cymbals, we can relate our dance to this cleansing of the "atmosphere" that surrounds us. The cheerful bell tones of the cymbals bring our most lyrical emotions out to play, and the high tones do wonders for your energy field. They can also burst the "bubbles" of negative thoughts, and clear the air. An enchanting dance with finger cymbals brings good vibrations, and I believe they can actually transmute hostility into bliss!

☞ To learn how to play with finger cymbals takes not only practice but technique. Find a teacher that can introduce you to this enchanting instrument (or come for one of my workshops!).

Swords Representing Ether

Dance researchers have not been able to show that the Sword Dance was common in history, but I have heard stories from many experienced traditional dancers that it was, and I believe them.

For instance, Maja "The Girl from The Nile," an Egyptian dancer now residing in Florida, once told me that there was a time in ancient history when dancers used to be sold as slaves into the courts or as a property of the wealthy. Some of them acclimated well, but some retained their independence in a very special way. They started dancing with swords normally used in battle. They did not use them fighting mode as the men did, but balanced them on their heads, expressing themselves: "You control my life, you hold the sword over my head, but you don't control my spirit." Maja says that Sword Dance is the masculine/feminine warrior within and the sword increases empowerment. (http://www.majanile.com)

Karen Andes, author of "Woman's Book of Balance," tells the story of the Dakinis, from the Hindu, Tibetan Buddhist and Tantric traditions. (http://www.worlddancefitness.com/index.html)

"Dakinis were considered "illumined" women - part human and part goddess. They were said to live on the earth and in the spirit realm. Dakinis were thought to fly naked through the highest levels of reality and therefore were called "sky-dancing women." They danced through the sky in ecstasy, embracing life. To entice, they wore sweet perfumes and flowers, carried essences of herbs, sang and chanted prayers, danced, performed mudras, (sacred hand gestures) carried a torch of heavenly white light and sometimes bestowed blessings and good fortune on others. But to shock, they wielded swords to cut people free from old entrapments, and they often devoured the bodies they killed."

Dancing with a sword can symbolize cutting through illusion. It is as if a great veil keeps us from seeing the true purpose of life. I visualize it as if the cosmos was polluted by a cloudy veil of dark emotions that limits us from seeing the truth, and only a sword can cut through this veil! Cut off illusion as you dance with your sword!

Try balancing the sword on your head, shoulders, hips, hands and arms. Hold it with both hands and move with it as if you were cutting curtains of unknown mysteries.

Just play with your intent and create different ways of dancing with the sword. Sometimes, I like to imagine that I am cutting off misunderstandings, false rules, hypocrisy and fear. I also enjoy contrasting the sharpness of the sword with the softness of my undulating and sinuous movements.

Cane Representing Air

Cane dance is part of the Middle Eastern Dance repertoire. The cane expresses joy, power or playfulness. The song is always very lyrical.

Here are stories that I have heard about the cane:

Delilah, a well known Belly Dancer from Seattle said:

"There is a special type of flute, called Ney, that is made of the same wood used to make the canes. The Ney is a very ancient instrument and was used in rituals and mystical practices. It is said to represent humans because it has the same number of orifices as the human body. The sound

of the Nay is very spiritual and its musical expressiveness comes through the breath, just as our lives do. The Sufis believe that the sound of the Ney communicates with God. It is said that the cane was also adopted by the Pharaohs for exoteric practices. Perhaps it was a sort of ancient Egyptian "magic wand," for it comes from the same material of the nay."

I like to dance with the cane as if it was my own personal "magic wand." I twirl and whirl the cane over my head and on the sides of my body, tossing and bouncing with it, as if making the transformational magic "from thin air" that I need for my life and those watching the dance. Try this magic wand dance and be receptive to what it says to you!

Water Jars Representing Water

In the Middle East and Southeast Asia, water jars are made of clay and are used to keep water cool without refrigeration. The people there say that water jars are never empty: when they are not holding water, they contain sound, because each jar shape has its own frequency.

They also believe that the jar is a symbolic representation of female energies, and therefore the creation. Since the jar is shaped like a womb, it has the potential to become "pregnant" with the potter's creative energy and give birth to any form.

Dancing while balancing a water jar on your head is very profound. It took clay, water and fire to make the pots. What better symbolism for all the elements at once, don't you think? Try out the water jar's "magic" with awareness and intent the next time you dance!

Think about this:

What is that I want to create in my life with this dance!

Now let's learn more about how we can represent the four elements by dancing with a veil.

Rosane Gibson

VEIL REPRESENTING THE FOUR ELEMENTS

To dance with the veil and to make the dance and the veil look beautiful and romantic requires concentration and imagination, poise and balance, awareness and sensitivity. You have to work with the veil tenderly and to be gentle with it and to put yourself in the veil as if you are the veil and as if the veil is you. You blend into each other and you create a limitless movement and the veil becomes like a wind playing with the waves of the sea, when the waves rise and fall tenderly impressing the wind and they feel the coolness on their cheeks and they fall down to the sea with joy and delight and they rise again for another tempting kiss.

Dancing with the veil will create vision after vision of imagination and flight to the depth of the reality where you are in an action meditation that knows nothing but the lushness and the living force of the moment. When you do justice to the veil, the veil will transcend to perfection. The veil symbolizes the many thousands of veils in the lives of the people of the world. The veil is a mystery and when you master the mystery of the veil you will be able to understand the secret of the phenomena of veils and the bondage that keep people hidden behind the invisible veils[7].

- Adnan Sarhan

---

[7] Reprinted with permission from Adnan Sarhan, Tantra Magazine Feb./March 1992

ENERGIZING AND PURIFIYING THE VEILS WITH THE ELEMENTS

I ritually energize my veils before dancing with them. By energizing the veil I become in tune with it, as if the prop and myself were one.

ENERGIZING EARTH

You can earth-energize your veil under a tree: Wrapping it around your back, stay there for a few minutes, breathing and communing with the earth. You could also use quartz crystals or salt, after folding your veil in a square and standing on it. Dance for the tree!

ENERGIZING FIRE

On a warm, sunny day, lay down in a meadow or lawn and cover your whole body with the veil; stay for a while, breathing and absorbing the solar energy. Take your veil to the beach and dance for the sun!

ENERGIZING AIR

When possible, I like to go to the top of a mountain and let the wind blow through the veil. I run around trailing my veils by a corner through the air; or simply jump and play in the wind with them. You can use your intuition: maybe you would like to energize your veil in front of a fan or waving it through incense smoke. Light the incense and dance with your veil, allowing the sacred aromas to permeate the cloth. I also had the exciting opportunity to energize my veils on hang gliders and ultra-light flights!

ENERGIZING WATER

Go out in the rain wrapped in your veil and enjoy the shower! Or go to a waterfall, or take a river bath holding the veils in your hands! Scent tap or spring water with perfumes or herbs and spray the veil with a vaporizer. Take your veil to the beach and dance for the waves in the ocean!

DANCING THE SUN AND THE MOON RHYTHMS WITH THE VEILS

As the sun and the moon play hide-and-seek in the sky, so may the rhythms of the dance! The rhythms that represent the sun are fast, strong and outgoing. The rhythms that represent the moon are slower, sensual, feminine and mysterious, like the moon.

- **Half Moon** – the dancer hides her body, hinting of the mystery to be revealed. Usually at the beginning of the song.
- **New Moon** – the dancer uses the veil as a frame around her constant undulating movements. Everything changes from moment to moment, as life can be a whole new experience if we allow it.
- **Full Moon** – dancing turns, spinning with the veil through the room, acknowledging abundance and prosperity in life. Everything we need will come to us if we surround to the moment.
- **Waxing Crescent Moon** - The dancer slows down her speed gradually until stopping. A time to focus inwards and connect to self feeling. Who am I? What I am doing here?
- **Waning Crescent Moon** – the dancer releases the veil, accelerating the movements as the flavor of the music changes. This shows the understanding of being one with all the mysteries, trusting the process of evolution. Go with the flow. Drop everything and just trust.

Dance with as many veils as you want. By assigning a symbol to each veil you will connect and bond with its symbolic meaning. Decide what each veil means to you, and create a dance that expresses that feeling. Or choose a symbol set, and decide how each veil could fit within it. For example, when I give meanings to each of my veils, I use the color chart as a guide (see page 140*). I have such symbols as the colors of the rainbow, the chakras of the body, my goals in life, and my problems to be released. Each veil you dance with can represent something of significance to you.

THE FIFTH ELEMENT: ETHER

In metaphysics, the fifth element takes the name of Akasha from that place in the astral plane where the akashic records are held, the accounting of all that has happened in the past, present, and future of the universe and beyond.

Akasha is actually an East Indian word meaning inner-space, reflecting the belief that the universe is both within and outside ourselves. Akasha means "the spiritual ether (or Aether); the omnipresent fifth occult element which embraces the other four- earth, air, fire, and water - and from which they manifest. This is the realm of "pattern" or causality, from which the five senses evolve. Some define it is the "other" of the "two worlds" that the witch or magician walks between.

In China, the Five Elements are used to tell fortunes, In Feng Shui they represent the phases of life, seasons of the year and personalities. It is said that when the seasons and environment change, the Five Elements have certain responses in human's behavior. The Taoist scholars made predictions about the human life cycle, from birth to death, by observing the natural properties of the five elements.

According to ancient Greek and Druidic philosophies, the elusive spiritual fifth element was called "ether" and was thought of as a binder that held everything in the universe together, often compared to a cargo ship or boat.

The Ethereal element has no direction, yet encompasses all directions. It is the center, the circumference, above and below. It is beyond seasons and time, yet is all seasons and time. It is the purely spiritual element, the realm of the All. It is protection and justice, movement and mastery, life and death and rebirth. Thus, ether is often symbolized by the turning wheel, or the sign of Infinity.

The fifth element is the dance itself. It is the interaction of all movements with or without any prop. It is looking beyond the body as a physical form. It is encompasses the whole self, beyond the parts. It is the spectrum of energy that perpetuates the dance into the eternity of the now... a sensory journey into mesmerizing movements that unfolds the mystery of who we are. In the etheric, the dancer becomes the dance.

Dance brings the necessary energy to cross the way, walking the paths to the unknown. That energy is in the drumming, the music, the dance, the happiness that involves everybody when we are doing or watching a dance. Weather dancing or watching the dancers, the ecstasy touches us the same, sooner or later, depending on our capacity to give ourselves totally to the present moment. This is the ether!

Open your heart to the rhythmic balance that is connected with the ether rhythm. When that rhythm, which touches everything everywhere, connects with our own rhythm, the body becomes pure joy, the senses open to the real and the sound of the drum encompasses the feast. Infinite love pours its sweetness over the entire group, as it moves, sings, dances, meditates and changes. We change from mechanical to creative, from boredom into exultation, sadness into joy, the robotic into the alive, above and beyond, eternal and forever. And this change is as irreversible as life itself.

Enlightening the Body

THE IMPORTANCE OF THE COSTUMES

The body is as important as the mind and it is the temple of the soul. We need to take good care of our bodies by eating well, exercising and grooming.

As in "real life," what your wear as a dancer sends a message to all who observe you. The clothing you wear to work or play in is also a costume. When we dress up to go to a party, it is quite different than when we dress for exercise. In the martial arts, uniforms convey the level of expertise of the student. In hospitals, we identify doctors and nurses by their uniforms. It is the same with priests and nuns, and soccer and baseball players. Dancing without a costume is like writing a poem with no verse, painting without colors, or composing a song without instruments. The costume completes your message. It is a visual representation of the story you tell with movement and music. The colors of the fabric, and the style and flow of the costume enhance what the dancer wants to expresses.

A costume is like the frame of a painting. Just as a frame can be ornate or simple, so can the costume. As a frame complements the artwork, the costume complements your dance and shows it to its best advantage. Costume defines your dance as a theatrical piece. It is a symbol and a tool for creativity and enriches the story told through dance. The costume can also be a healing tool through its colors and fabrics.

It is also *fun* to wear costumes! It can be a playful and highly creative experience. By using different fabrics and colors, we can intuitively promote healing and a feeling of bliss. It is like awakening our inner child to play.

"I would like to suggest that you create your own costume to dance. Get inspirations from costume books, magazines or observe other dancers. Always look for something that will make you wonderfully beautiful!"

Rosane Gibson

ENLIGHTENMENT THROUGH THE COLORS

According to Ayurvedic practitioners Venkat and Christine Machiraju, our light body, which reflects the chakra system, can be healed with light and color, and is in fact made up of the spectrum of colors of the rainbow. They say:

"Everywhere in nature we see beautiful combinations of color – green leaves and stems, pink flowers, blue sky, red berries, purple sunsets, orange fruits.. So many colors! The rainbow that is seen in the sky after a summer shower is duplicated in our astral bodies – by the chakras, which are wheels of color (see page 49*). The organs, which correspond to the chakras on the physical body are healed and cleansed by the color of the chakra that they are associated with. The moods and emotions can also be changed with color and often times we associate colors with emotions. Red is for anger, blue represents a cool personality, pink is for health, etc."

Colors have profound affects on the wearer and the beholder, and they have several modes of application. Color can be therapeutic. Meditating on colored flowers is a good way to brighten the mind. The use of colored crystals applied to specific parts of the body can clear energy blocks. Exposure to different colored lights or surroundings can have a healing effect. Simply incorporating color in your home or office environment also has an important effect. Color should be considered when buying a new car, clothing or home to make sure that you are bringing the energy into your life that suits you.

We can consciously pick colors for their specific healing and empowering properties when choosing costumes, draping fabric for a set design, setting up a stage backdrop or painting the room we perform in. Let's take a look at specific colors and the meaning they hold.

RED

Red is an earth color and corresponds to the zodiacal signs of Taurus, Capricorn and Virgo. Vibrant and vigorous in tone, red promotes energy and sensuality. It also represents Mars and martial, warlike energy. Red is also related to the material world, assisting in the acquisition of physical needs (because it is the color of the root chakra, which governs survival). If you are seeking a better-structured life, security, or more energy, wear red to make it happen. When used, it is reassuring, and can remove repressed feelings. Red strengthens the heart and blood circulation. It can be a very stimulating color. When combined with black it creates an aggressive quality.

ORANGE

Orange is related to the element water and corresponds to the zodiac signs of Cancer, Scorpio and Pisces. Orange activates the body systems, and is good for general health. It is recommended for those who are frequently ill, lack vitality, and have weak muscles (or weak will power). It also helps cultivate generosity, expansiveness, self-respect, creativity and reproduction. If someone is looking for a healthier body, wants to conceive, or feels jealous and insecure, wearing orange will help overcome these challenges. Orange is energizing. It is good for the uterus, thyroid, and bladder. As well, it is indicated for clearing blocks that cause stagnation and paralysis. Orange can be used to increase creativity.

YELLOW

Yellow is related to the element fire and the sun, and correspond to the zodiac signs of Sagittarius, Leo and Aries. Particularly related to the stomach area, (where the yellow "solar plexus" chakra is seated), yellow is a good color for digestion. Wearing yellow and gold promotes enthusiasm and happiness. They also help to change feelings of anger, impatience, annoyance, and laziness. Yellow and gold help us become more dynamic, yet tolerant. Yellow is great for the nervous system and brain. It is also a good color for healing the kidneys. It increases energy and creates movement. It is very helpful in treating pain related to arthritis. Yellow is a clarifying color, and thus is good for opening up lines of communication. Used in excess, yellow can make one hyperactive.

GREEN

Green is related to the element air and corresponds to the zodiac signs of Aquarius, Gemini and Libra. Green promotes self-expression, communication, serenity and calmness. It is prescribed to calm down stressful and confused thoughts. Like Nature herself, green brings balance, peace and harmony (corresponding to the heart chakra). It is a harmonizing color, and calming to mind and nerves. It is used in healing the liver, spleen and pituitary gland. It has a soothing effect on all fire problems: fever, acidity and hyperactivity.

SKY BLUE

This color relates to the element ether. It helps release tension and energy blocks. Blue relaxes the body and projects fluidity to our movements, making them more delicate. It is advised for those who have a long-winded or argumentative personality. Sky blue opens the mind, bringing a willingness to listen and discuss by freeing tension. It is related to the throat chakra. It helps reduce tumors, congestion, fevers and infections. It is used for the eyes and pineal gland. It reduces anger and hatred. Used in excess light blue can make one cool and unfeeling.

DARK BLUE or INDIGO

Dark blue promotes concentration and detachment, and clears the mind. This color is also mysterious, and is advised for those who are very extroverted and need more discretion. It also makes the dance movements more sublime.

PURPLE

Purple is a color that creates an aura of prestige. It is good for reducing cysts, heart pain and stiffness. It is also considered royal or spiritual.

VIOLET

Violet is a color that increases devotion. It is very good for rooms where meditation is practiced. It builds white blood cells in the spleen. This is a color that promotes spiritual growth. Violet is excellent for people who suffer from AIDS, hepatitis, cancer, lupus and other immune diseases.

WHITE

White is a nurturing color. It is a pure color and is the best to wear to perform any spiritual activity. It is a healing color and this is why it is universally warn in hospitals. It counteracts fevers and infections, calms the mind, heart and nerves, and soothes the emotions. If used excessively, white can be suppressing to the emotions or make one feel inhibited, lazy or hypersensitive.

Both violet and white are colors associated with pure consciousness, vision and insight (and the crown chakra). They open us intuitively to higher guidance, and thus make our dance movements smooth and graceful. They access creativity and promote a state of inner peace and wisdom.

SILVER

The color silver evokes the lunar (moon) emotions of romance and inspiration. It is associated with water. It relaxes and helps release tension, and is recommended for busy people coping with many responsibilities. Silver promotes femininity, encourages receptivity and creates a bit of mystery. Using silver costumes will lend a flowing effect to your dance.

GOLD

Gold invokes the sun. It is related to passion and action. The color gold increases the strength of the heart and immune system and balances endocrine or hormone functions. It is a warming color for the body. On a spiritual level, Gold increases awareness, purity and virtue. When used in dance, it improves the shimmies!

PINK

Pink is good for people who are very intellectual and rational, egocentric or cold, and want to bring out their emotional side. This color helps activate feelings of compassion and love towards others and self.

DARK PINK

Dark pink helps strengthen emotions, and promotes security and happiness. It is recommended for fragile personalities, such as those who cry easily and are overly sensitive.

BROWN

Brown is a grounding and stabilizing color. It should not be used as a primary color in a room as it does not promote thought or spiritual growth. It is good to use brown when you are spacing out or losing material belongings. Brown and red are good for money.

BLACK

Black is a color that lets no light pass through it. It tends to create depression and obstruction. Black is not a negative color though; you can use the healing powers of black when you want to avoid interference from others' energies into your own. It blocks any other color or energy interference. Psychically, black absorbs all colors (as opposed to white, which reflects).

Be aware of the colors that are around you.

Look in your closet and observe which colors are your clothes. Ask yourself if you have a tendency to like one color more then the other, or if there is any color that you really don't like. Ask yourself why.

Be open for the healing power of the colors.

Be in the Moment

ENLIGHTENMENT DANCE
How Dance Can Improve the Way You Think, Feel, and Live

THE STORY OF THE MONK AND THE STRAWBERRIES
(Traditional Parable)

Once upon a time there was a monk running away from a big bear, up on a mountain. He was running as fast as he could since the bear would surly kill him. The Monk got to the edge of the cliff and then he had to choose: to jump or not to jump?

He jumped, and as he was falling down, he grabbed a branch of tree that was sticking out, and held on to keep from falling. He thought he was saved, but he looked down to see how far he was from the ground and although he was not too far, there was a wild tiger below. He then looked to the left side, only to find out that a pack of wild rats were starting to bite the tree branch he was holding himself on. He thought: "wow, up there the big bear, down there the wild tiger and here I have these rats."

Behind the branch he saw a little strawberry bush with a large strawberry fruit on it, ready to be eaten. He appreciated the opportunity and reached out to taste the delicious fruit! Ah, delicious!

Moral:

The Bear - represents our past problems - it is there up on the hill, it is not going to catch him anymore!

The Tiger – represents our future problems. Many things could have happened with the tiger. He could have slept, or he could have left to chase a prayer, or a hunter could have killed him, many things can happen to the future… so don't worry about it!

The wild Rats: represent the present circumstances. Bills to pay, work to do, worries of the present. They too can overdose us with fear. Many things could have happened with the rats.

The strawberry – represents the magic that is existent only in the present moment. The present moment is the now, the moment of the breath. Keep the present moment in focus and you will only find strawberries in your life!

ENLIGHTENMENT DANCE
How Dance Can Improve the Way You Think, Feel, and Live

JUST DANCE!

Sometimes I see people resist dancing. It is not uncommon to hear: "I have no rhythm," "I have no coordination," "I can't dance," "I am too old," "There's not enough room to dance," "I don't have the energy to dance right now," "I am too shy, I only dance at home, alone, and I can't dance in front of people!" "No, I hate my body.." and so on...

Dance has been part of human culture since its inception! It is in our DNA. Our ancestors danced; dance is present in every tribe; every child knows how to dance, some of us even before we were born.. kicking and punching in the womb in rhythm with the music! Why do we learn to make excuses to avoid one of the most natural things our body wants to do?

I notice dance everywhere in peoples' lives. I see their bodies dressed all the same, in robot-like suits, while their feet are tapping the floor under the table. I see hands drumming absent-mindedly on the counter, while waiting for their food at the snack bar. I see ears listening to a Walkman while their owner walks in rhythm with the music. I find rhythm in conversation, in the movement of the stars, the seasons of the earth. Everything is dancing! The birds, butterflies and bees… they dance in their flights! Trees sway in the wind while oceans beat against the shore, composing this ecstatic dance of the planet and the universe!

If you pay careful attention, you will feel the dance too -- the rhythms that make up your life. You will find the dancer that is within you! You don't need to be a professional, trained dancer to be able to dance. You can express yourself through dance in a very spontaneous way, using your movements to tell stories of your daily life and expressing your feelings and emotions.

Pay attention to these rhythms, and let your body express the world's (nature's) music. Tell stories with your body, letting the music be your guide. Dance as if you were a painter, and your limbs were your paintbrushes. Imagine your life stories, memories from the past, ideas for the future, people you have met, people you know now, and interpret this through your dance! Imagine that your audience is able to see and feel the vision that you are bringing to the music.

Here are some more ideas to get you started: Dance the caring side of your personality. Dance your responsible side. Dance your irresponsible side. Dance your holy and sacred side. Dance your sexual side. Dance your wisdom. Dance your fears. Dance your passions. Dance you anger. Dance your happiness. Dance your sadness. Dance your compassion. Dance your ancestry. Dance like an animal. Dance a conversation.

Create gestures for your dance, with your own unique meanings; a personal dictionary of dance moves to add to your dance vocabulary. There are infinite gestures we perform in our day-to-day life -- for instance: praying, searching, finding, sharing, blessing, offering, receiving, guiding, playing an instrument, hugging your lover, combing your hair, saying hello or goodbye, sewing, cooking, holding the baby, making copies, talking on the phone, using the Internet.

The physical movements we make as we do these things can all be formalized into elegant, graceful, and meaningful dance movements that express the small moments that make up all our lives. Life is a dance. Please feel inspired to create your own Enlightenment Dance (or sign up for classes or workshops that may be happening around your area*).

DANCE YOUR LIFE

The Universe is full of rhythms. There is a rhythm for each season of the year. Spring has a different rhythm than summer. The rhythms in the city differ from the rhythms of the mountains. The planets perform an entire choreography around the Sun. Each one of us has a rhythm that dances in harmony with the rhythms of the Universe. There is a rhythm to our walk, to our talk, to our gestures, to our jogging, to our dance.

Our conversations with people also have their own rhythms. All of us together have rhythms that are in harmony with each other and with the Universe. Life is simpler when we hear, feel, and understand these rhythms. The infinite intelligence of the Universe is behind these rhythms. As we become more sensitive to them, we pick up the natural guidance that is there for us at all times.

If you pay attention to the events of your life, you will see that they happen according to rhythms. When you don't agree with someone it is because your rhythms are not the same. Even though there is love, you might not be "dancing" to the same beat! On the other hand, when you adore someone and it is reciprocated, that is because your rhythms are perfectly in sync.

New York City has a different rhythm then Miami Beach. Soccer has a different rhythm then volleyball. Belly Dance has a different rhythm then Jazz. Women have different rhythms then men. The lesson here is to learn to dance all the rhythms! By this I mean, *go with the flow*, whether it is salsa, flamenco or rock and roll!

DANCE YOUR INNER DANCE!

The human world of illusion, with its typical disregard for what is natural, simple, and easy, creates so much background noise that we often do not hear or feel the underlying rhythms. But we can choose to create more quiet in our lives in order to restore these basic rhythms.

Our increased sensitivity to rhythm creates a more peaceful environment in our lives. As a result, we will have a deeper appreciation for the magnificent harmony that is always present in the Universe. Take time to be quiet; to be still. Just listen and you'll hear the rhythms. Feel the inner dance.

DANCE TO CONNECT WITH OTHERS!

One of the ways we complicate our lives is by thinking of ourselves as separate from each other and from the Universe. So strong is this belief that we must continually remind ourselves that each of us is an integral part of a universal experience and that our individual power derives from this connectedness. The more we open ourselves to the inherent perfection in everything just the way it is, the more fun we have. The easier it becomes for each of us to surrender to the love in ourselves and everyone else, the richer and fuller is our life experience.

Dancing in a group is a form of healing and understanding our unity. Group dance has been performed since the beginnings of time! The Hopi elders say: *"At this time in history, we are to take nothing personally, least of all ourselves, for the moment we do, our spiritual growth and journey come to a halt. The Way of the Lone Wolf is over, Gather yourselves."* Look for friends that like to dance and create your own dance community!

DANCE TO FEEL ALIVE!

The opportunity to live our lives is the greatest privilege we have. Like any privilege, it must first be cherished in order to be enjoyed.

Every time we open our hearts to another, we exercise this privilege and learn again what a magnificent gift life is. We can only feel life fully if we focus our attention on the quality of life we desire. Quality of life is the setting for the events and people that pass through our lives.. people that we share moments with. By dancing, we can achieve the joy of feeling alive through allowing ourselves to intertwine with others. Our bodies can express movements that call out through the layers of judgments and repressed feelings. Dancing peels these layers off and uncovers the joy allowing us to fill our being with eternal bliss!

DANCE TO MAKE LOVE!

Dance can be wonderful foreplay for lovers! It creates a spiritual connection that must precede the physical for successful intimacy. I encourage you to experience it.. whether dancing for your partner or with him (or her). Be inventive with props such as feathers, scarves, and veils.

Christina Sophia, a dancer in the Tantric spiritual tradition (www.tantradance.com) has developed a unique style which she calls "sacred-erotic belly dance." She says:

"Dance is one of the arts mentioned in the Kama Sutra, the classical Indian book on the Art of Love. It is suggested that men and women alike should be well versed in these arts. Tantric ritual involves a weaving together of these arts into an expansive, ecstatic experience. Ancient ecstasy teachings recognized the harmonizing ability of sacred dance. Natural movements and gestures mirrored by the partners engaged in a sacred dance can harmonize mood and overcome the sense of separation and the limitations of personality.

Sacred-erotic dance is as the words suggest, movement that is earthy, sensual and erotic which is natural for the body, yet it is coming from a very deep place within that is 'felt into' so that we may experience ourselves in connection and harmony with the universe, ourselves, our bodies. We begin with the intention to move from our spirit, our source and our heart and to be fully in the present. This is a powerful meditation and healing to do just with ourselves. With a partner, it can be a loving and passionate way to connect energetically, harmonize moods, and enjoy the creative flow of moving together sensually. Eye gazing and breathing together align your energies and open the way to deeper ecstatic experiences. Allow yourself, alone or with a partner to experiment. Free yourselves, there is no right or wrong way to move! It is simply a spontaneous expression in the moment from your heart into the heart of all, which you and your beloved are part of.

You may wish to try sacred-erotic dance with your partner or on your own. After setting the mood and your intention for the ritual, put on some "sacred-erotic" music that especially moves you. It can be very fun and enchanting to begin your ritual this way adding touch and eye gazing if partnered, to your movement. I've discovered through interacting with my partner this way in performance and private ritual that we have become attuned to one another in many subtle ways. Dance is an opening into uncharted, multi-dimensional realms of communication, connection and expression which are truly ecstatic!"

Pick a song that you both love! Or a very sensual one that moves you! Dress up very sexy and dance for him / her. I encourage you to dance passionate dance movements that come from your heart and soul! I guarantee you will mesmerize and fascinate your lover with this enlightening experience!

DANCE TO PLAY!

When we were young we imagined there were fairies in the pond. We used to hide beneath the bed, climb trees, and to believe in our dreams! Every moment was an adventure; the world was full of wonder and play! Then we grew up. The fairies moved away. We took business reports to bed and stopped playing.

In the adult world, there seems to be little room for playtime. When we do take time off work, we call it "leisure" or "sport" and work too hard at that too: going to the gym to lose weight, competing at sports to win the game, drinking ourselves silly as we desperately try to relax. And do we feel better? Hardly.

Why do we cease to play? Psychologist Ann Marie Woodall says the conditioning starts very young. *"We are taught as kids to be careful, to watch out, so the world out there becomes frightening and serious. As we grow up, that idea becomes lodged and makes us scared of letting go and playing."*

Many therapists and psychologists say that the best thing we could do is to relearn how to play. It is not a case of being childish, but rather of seeing the world from a childlike perspective – as a place of endless wonder and joy. I have learned to look deeply into each student's eyes and mentally ask: *where is your inner child that came out to play with me today?*

The music, the costumes, the stories and the enlightening insights you will have when you dance will release your wise inner child, who is just waiting for a chance to come out to play the guru of your life. Let your spirit shine through your entire body! Refuse to get old! "Don't give years to your life, but rather give life to your years!" Don't buy into social standards about what to wear and how to behave when you reach a certain age. Be alive! Be yourself; show off your soul! By allowing yourself to shine, you permit others to do the same.

Dance Your Way To Bliss!

Enlightenment Dance Students' Stories

ENLIGHTENMENT DANCE
How Dance Can Improve the Way You Think, Feel, and Live

Kimberly Hanson:

Enlightenment dance has become part of who I am, not just something that I do.

I began my journey with Enlightenment Dance and it's talented, gorgeous and inspirational creator Rosane, a little over a year ago. My journey is still in its infancy and I am looking forward to a lifelong trip in which I will grow. If I had to describe what Enlightenment Dance means to me in just three words, those words would be; Health, Fun and Empowerment.

I knew I was dying. Okay, I wasn't going to drop dead right away, but there were signs. Elevated blood pressure, a persistent cough, constant fatigue, gripping muscle spasms, overwhelming feelings of stress and irritability. I felt much older than I was and not only was my health declining, but I felt miserable inside too.

The day I met Rosane, I did so timidly. I was ashamed of my weight, my body, myself. I covered the center of my shame, my tummy strategically in layers of clothing. I pulled my skirt up high almost to my nipple line and then on top of that I added a long shirt, which I cinched in with a thick scarf tied well above my waistline. I folded my arms in front of my tummy, and I was ready to begin my first belly dance lesson!

*Learning to dance with Rosane has helped me to slowly strip away those protective layers. Not just the outer layers of clothing, but also the inner layers of negative thinking, self-doubt and shame. I have a newly found sense of self-acceptance. Rosane has a special gift for helping others to heal through dance. Sure, I do not yet have the body I would like to have, but I have learned to be more grateful for the body that I **do** have. I am learning to love my tummy! I am so happy that my body is allowing me to learn to dance. I am thrilled that I have the opportunity to share in that dance with other females who are so supportive, non-judgmental and truly "sisters in dance." As a group, this "sisterhood" is a positive move towards the* *empowerment of women, while learning to be comfortable with femininity.*

Enlightenment dance has given me tremendously improved mental and physical health. It is so much fun!

Kimberly Hanson

Sylvia Partain

Aging is not graceful, unless of course, you determine that it will be. I was once a dancer, and I choreographed and taught dance and drill teams for fifteen years. Then I took a different course in my career and I retired from dance, never giving a thought to "use it or lose it." Twenty years later, at age 60, I lost my tenacity for working out, so I again looked at dance as an exercise that would make that hour pass with a helluva lot more fun. But my knees were now gone, my body wouldn't follow directions, and balance had disappeared completely. I now used the rail going upstairs and a step-at-a-time coming down.

I timidly signed up for Rosane's belly dance class and immediately became infatuated with the teacher's enthusiasm. There were others younger and older, and everyone was friendly. Rosane introduced a whole new world of mind and body and I looked forward to each Monday night. After nine months of fun exercise embedded with inspiration and creativity, I noticed the strength I had gained in the muscles surrounding my knees. Going up and down stairs--no problem. Balance--it's beginning to return. Creativity--it's a new me!

Sylvia Partain - "Amyrillis"

Christine Praria

Rosane brought spirit into my dance, and helped me find the confidence to dance without choreography, from the heart and soul. After my first private lesson with this beautiful, exotic, fiery woman I knew I had found a teacher who could help me grow spiritually through dance. I was exhilarated!

ENLIGHTENMENT DANCE
How Dance Can Improve the Way You Think, Feel, and Live

Gypsy dance focuses largely around the dancer's flashy, flowing skirts, but what makes the moves and the costume work is the free-spirited and spontaneous attitude of the gypsy. Rosane taught me about getting into that spirit, finding freedom in my heart and joy in my body and dancing with wild abandon. None of my teachers had ever taken a spiritual approach before.

With Rosane I learned to draw on feminine earth energies, circulating them through my body and allowing them to find expression through the power of the gypsy persona. She taught me to flirt, to pose, to be passionately angry as well as deliriously joyous, to compete, to cooperate, and most of all to enjoy my body and lose myself in the music, letting it flow through me.

My breakthrough came after performing my first solo for an audience. Because of my nerves and a wet floor I forgot my choreography and was forced to improvise, to dance spontaneously. I realized I didn't need choreography. In the alchemical marriage of the internalized moves and the free spirit of the persona I was able to let my body take over.

Now when I dance, I feel ecstasy, just from interacting with the music and feeling each movement flow effortlessly into the next. It is an active meditation, as I let go of conscious control and trust my body and skills to create something beautiful.

I love Rosane -- she has such glorious goddess energy, a beautiful body and a radiant, loving spirit. She showed me a path to enlightenment that never would have occurred to me, and it has made dance not only an exercise or artistic outlet for me; it is a truly spiritual experience.

Christine Praria, Orlando/ FL

BIBLIOGRAPHY

Alexander, Jane. The Natural Year Bantam Books

Andes, Karen. A Woman's Book of Strength, A Woman's Book of Power, The Berkley Publishing Group, (Penguin Putnam Inc.)

Andes, Karen. A Woman's Book of Balance The Berkley Publishing Group, (Penguin Putnam Inc.)

Andes, Karen, A Woman's Book of Power - The Berkley Publishing Group, (Penguin Putnam Inc.)

Brown, Lonny PhD. Enlightenment in Our Time www.BookLocker.com/LonnyBrown

Buenaventura, Wendy The Serpent of The Nile

Cober, Harold Theodynamics Luthers, New Smyrna Beach, FL 32168-6221

Djoumahna, Kajira The Tribal Bible PO Box 14926, Santa Rosa, CA 95402

Gupta, Roxanne Kamayani, PhD A Yoga of Indian Classical Dance Inner Traditions International

Hay, Louise L You Can Heal Your Life Hay House, Inc.

Richards, Tazz The Belly Dance Book - Backbeat Press

Redmond, Layne When The Drummers Were Women

Roth, Gabrielle. Sweat Your Prayers: Movement as a Spiritual Practice. New York: J.P. Tarcher/ Putnam, 1997.

Roth, Gabrielle Maps to Ecstasy Nataraj Publishing

Stewart, Iris J Sacred Woman, Sacred Dance - Inner Traditions International

Vajra Ma. The Tantric Dance of Feminine Power. Woman Mysteries of The Ancient Future Sisterhood. PO Box 39A59 LA, CA 90039

Wong, Eva A Master Course in Feng Shui Shambhala

ABOUT THE AUTHOR

Rosane Gibson is an emerging voice in the field of personal transformation. She is a dance artist, teacher, coach, entrepreneur and philanthropist. Rosane uses a contemporary somatic approach involving weightless body movement, dance and poetry to help her clients overcome challenges and live to their fullest potential.

Rosane is a real-life example of applying self-actualization techniques for life transformation. In the middle of a divorce, working full time, and raising three sons, she envisioned a life with much greater purpose. She decided to follow her calling and move in an entirely different direction.

During her transformation she wrote a book "How to Mend Your Broken Heart", retired from her corporate career, and moved to Sedona, Arizona, where she now offers retreats and outdoors life coaching experiences. Rosane also works with clients globally through online sessions.

To learn more about her workshops, talks, and offerings, please go to RosaneGibson.com